Secon

Navtej Sarna's fictional wo and *We Weren't Lovers Lik* collection *Winter Evenings* .... includes the historical travel narrative on Jerusalem *Indians at Herod's Gate* and the translation of the *Zafarnama*. He contributes regularly to the *Times Literary Supplement*, *Financial Times* and other journals.

As a career diplomat, he has served as the Foreign Office Spokesman and as India's envoy to Israel, United Kingdom and, most recently, to the United States.

Praise for *Second Thoughts*

'Navtej Sarna carries on the noble tradition of the writer-diplomat, like Nobel Prize-winning poets Pablo Neruda and Saint-John Perse before him.' – Michael Dirda, *The Washington Post*

'[A] fitting introduction to the world of classics – and those who made it possible.' – Shivam Saini, *Business Standard*

'It is an engaging collection, one that rides on nostalgia.' – Ziya Us Salam, *The Hindu*

Second Thoughts

Books by the same author

Folk Tales of Poland
We Weren't Lovers Like That
The Book of Nanak
The Exile
Zafarnama (trans.)
Winter Evenings
Savage Harvest (trans.)
Indians at Herod's Gate

Second Thoughts

On Books, Authors and the Writerly Life

NAVTEJ SARNA

HarperCollins *Publishers* India

First published in hardback in India by
HarperCollins *Publishers* in 2015
A-75, Sector 57, Noida, Uttar Pradesh 201301, India
www.harpercollins.co.in

This edition published in paperback in India in 2018 by HarperCollins *Publishers*

2 4 6 8 10 9 7 5 3 1

P-ISBN: 978-93-5302-404-8
E-ISBN: 978-93-5177-053-4

Typeset in 11/16 Warnock Pro
by Jojy Philip, New Delhi 110 015

Printed and bound at
Thomson Press India Ltd.

To my mother, Surjit Sarna

Contents

Introduction

What is it about writers and their stories? asked my companion of a drizzly afternoon in Dublin after we had hoofed around for a couple of hours through the lanes encircling Trinity College and had finally settled down in a pub. The perplexity behind the question was genuine. What indeed was the reason that had me staring with child-like fascination at a glass door that said that here is where Joyce met his future wife. Very future, actually – they lived together for nearly thirty years 'in sin', as it was called in Ireland those days. Or hang around reverentially at their assignation point on a street corner, doubly blessed as this is the same corner where stands the house in which Oscar Wilde lived for twenty-three of his forty-six years and across which he now sits in stony languid splendour in the dripping park. What is it that makes grown men jostle for space with tour groups so that they can be photographed against a window display of Joyce memorabilia at Sweny pharmacy of *Ulysses* fame? Or stare at the green brown blue glass bottles of early twentieth century chemistry inside the shop, nervously fingering a cake of lemon soap, a replica of the one that Leopold Bloom buys in the book?

And then, of course, we had not settled down in just any old pub – it was the pub where Bloom, the wandering Ulysses, settled down for a sandwich of gorgonzola cheese with mustard, accompanied by a glass of red burgundy.

It was not simply the chasing of literary celebrity, I concluded, though that is part of the answer. More substantially, it was a desire to understand the mind of the writer and the process of literary creation. A curiosity to know what influenced the great characters and stories of literature, what part of reality was turned into fiction, or how indeed successful fictional figures walk into real-life situations. This place where the real and the fictional world mingle is a fascinating one and here we don't seem to know – or in fact, care – whether it was Joyce who came into Sweny's or Bloom, whether Wilde lived in that corner house or Dorian Gray. Here we can be forgiven for being convinced that Sherlock Holmes actually lived in the house on Baker Street that thousands throng to and Hemingway was the old man who struggled with the big fish on the open sea.

This curiosity about the writer's mental landscape, the yearning for a whiff of the alchemy of inspiration, has governed many of my journeys over the last three decades and more and many of the pieces in this collection are the result. While travel to unusual places is fortunately part of my job, the writer in me has always tried to convert it to literary travel. By carrying, for instance, the right book in my handbag – the *Baburnama* to Kabul, *Lost Horizon* to Leh, Lermontov to Moscow – along with a wire-bound journal to take notes in. Or by chasing down famous literary haunts, be they pubs or graves. And then writing it all down in hotel rooms in faraway places, or in airport lounges, or while watching the rain blow fiercely in from the sea for three days without a stop, or staring at the peak with the temple at the top.

Sometimes the engagement with the subject has been direct – a sunny lunch over white wine with Mario Vargas Llosa, valuable friendships with Amos Oz and Eli Amir, a talk by Paul Theroux followed by a conversation, a drink with Khushwant Singh in his sunset years, listening to Ian McEwan in Jerusalem, a walk in the garden of a Soviet Communist Party hospital with Faiz Ahmad Faiz.

At other times the chase has been more tangential. Such as that grey, snow-bound weekend in 1983 when a few of us set off from Soviet Moscow for Yasnaya Polyana, Tolstoy's estate. Here, this prophet-like figure had accurately mapped the finely nuanced emotions of the Russian heart, mind and soul. And it was this estate that he left forever, drawn by the demons of his mind, ten days before his death, to die in the tiny house of a station master. But we were not to make it; we did not have the requisite permit that would allow foreigners to leave Moscow's city limits. Our entreaties to the Russian soul that we thought must reside somewhere in the Soviet guard who sat warm against the cold in his cubicle, a few eggs boiling in a saucepan beside him, were to no avail. So you will find no piece on Tolstoy and his surroundings in this collection.

I thought my chase of Ernest Hemingway would end in similar failure when a long planned trip to his house in Key West, Florida, fell through at the last moment. But I did catch up with him in Cuba and drank daiquiris and mojitos in the bars he used to frequent. Then I even made it to Finca Vigia, a farm outside Havana, first rented by his third wife Martha and converted to a comfortable home by her successor, Mary. Complete with his fishing boat *El Pillar*, his study, tennis court and pool, his hunting trophies, jackets and shoes and the graves of his four favourite dogs. Now, every time I pick up a Hemingway book, it is impossible not to recall his obsessive daily noting of his weight in pencil on his bathroom wall.

In 2008 I located Café Ali Baba over Cairo's Tahrir square where Naghib Mahfouz sat for decades with his breakfast, watching the changing face of life in the square, since made famous by the Arab Spring. But I was too late; the café was boarded up prior to its ultimate and unfortunate conversion into a fast-food joint. So I had to be satisfied with the El Fishawy café in the old bazaar, with its rounded tables and smudged carved mirrors, also visited at times by Mahfouz. In the magical meeting place of water, land and sky that is St Petersburg, I thought I saw Gogol's clerk in a threadbare overcoat hurrying along in the cold on Nevsky Prospekt and Pushkin's Bronze Horseman coming in pursuit down the bridge with open arms. I sat in the lobby of Chelsea Hotel, New York, expecting Leonard Cohen to walk in any moment, guitar in hand, or Jack Kerouac or Dylan Thomas. And then I walked down to the village to the White House Tavern where legend has it Thomas drank eighteen straight whiskeys and died. Compared to all this, the meeting with Wodehouse in his school at Dulwich was easy; a polite student received and escorted me to the Wodehouse library, complete with his pipe, his typewriter and personal copies of his books, where I was left to communicate in silence with the master.

Often the final resting place of the author has proved to be an ineluctable lodestone. The first such search, on Easter day in 1983, was for the grave of Boris Pasternak in the writers' retreat of Peredelkino, a few miles out of Moscow. The first few enquiries – people those days would recall him only as a poet and not as the author of the banned *Doctor Zhivago* – drew blank stares and a helpless shrugging of the shoulders. A few old women, swathed in overcoats and scarves, coming out of a heavy wooden church, were less circumspect. What one of them said has haunted me since: 'Look for the three pines'. We found the three pines in a thicket of white birch trees at the edge of the village and under those we found Pasternak's grave. Hand-painted Easter eggs lay at his feet, an odd tribute in a communist era, and yet so typical of Russia. The column that I wrote much later was triggered by a chance news snippet in the winter of 2006 that Pasternak's grave had been vandalized in Russia.

Chasing Graham Greene through Antibes, Vienna, Havana was exciting and not too difficult. But in death he had me flummoxed; he was not where he was supposed to be resting, according to a mistaken lead, in the Corsier village cemetery below the Swiss town of Vevey, in the company of Charlie Chaplin. In the mid-nineties I finally found grave number 528 in another cemetery altogether, in the neighbouring village of Corseaux. A grey cat stared suspiciously from behind the tombstone; blue crocuses and a rose bush, covered with fine powdery snow, were the only ostentation around the grave of a man who had made an art of studying human morality and frailty. Similarly I did not find Scott Fitzgerald in the place where he was buried in 1940. The golden boy of the jazz age, about whom it was said that he could write a bad book but could never write badly, had been moved, along with wife Zelda, by their daughter to the family plot at St Mary's Church in Rockville where they had been refused burial earlier for not being proper Catholics. The epitaph on his headstone – the last line from *The Great Gatsby*: 'So we beat on, boats against the current, borne back ceaselessly into the past' – adds a resonant poignancy both to the grave and to the book itself. And there are tales here of other resting places – those of Saadi and Hafiz in Shiraz, visited by dervishes and newly-weds, and that of Babur under the blue sky on the hillside above Kabul, surrounded by the fruit trees that he loved.

None of this, of course, would make any sense if it were not for the books, for the wondrous world that these men and women whom we admire and chase, in life and sometimes in death, have given us.

Nowadays it's easy to get hold of books. You can download them on your smart phone or have them delivered to your doorstep on cash-on-delivery basis. But none of this has the excitement of the roulette that one plays in a second-hand bookshop. I was bitten by the bug of the random find in the sixties in a little wooden shack in Dehradun, owned by a genial man who had a striking resemblance to Wodehouse himself. From him we bought a pile of Classics Illustrated and when he acquired more, we bought those too. And we found a binder close by who made convenient volumes for us. Julius Caeser and Puck, Cyrano de Bergerac and Saladin, Puddn'head Wilson, Jane Eyre, Heathcliff and Silas Marner and dozens more became familiar figures. Years later, that wooden shack featured in one of the first *Second Thoughts* columns; I owe more to it perhaps than to any library for whatever knowledge of the classics I possess. Second-hand bookshops have continued to fascinate and enchant since: one can only search in vain for the formula that could explain how a hundred-year-old volume of Keats can be lying next to a Perry Mason. I have hunted and haunted these shops wherever I could, from Paris to Pakistan, from Tel Aviv to Toronto, from Boston to Bangalore.

Bought in these treasure vaults or bought new or

received as thoughtful gifts, the books line up on the bookshelves, piling up horizontally when the vertical space is not enough. Looking through them is like finding companions from lost years; each recalls a different phase of one's life. The massive *Gone With the Wind* was finished mostly while standing against a pole in a crowded 'Univ Special' bus in 1974; *Lost Horizon* and *Random Harvest* are forever associated with the smell of talcum powder and the feel of summer kurtas in shaded college libraries a year later; Graham Greene's *An End of an Affair* was my only saviour in a PWD guest house in a small hill district capital in 1981 until I found the virginal fiction shelves of the local library; *Billiards at Nine* takes me back to my days of learning the game from a district dentist in a small club in the hills; *Lolita* seemed the most appropriate book to begin my stint in Moscow with, in the distant fall of 1982, and nearly three decades later Amos Oz's *The Black Box* would introduce me to Israel.

Many of the books that I read have strange scribblings in pencil on the blank pages at the end, especially some of the Greene and Maugham books, both of whom are regarded as writer's writers. Someone may surmise from these notings that the books were being summarized chapter-wise for a test; actually, this was the work of a struggling writer trying to figure out how the masters constructed a novel, how a character was introduced, how viewpoints changed and so on. I don't know if it helped much in the end except to convince me of something I already knew – that it was all very hard work. And so it proved to be, the learning of the craft step by step, uphill all the way. Yet it has been a journey that I would not have given up for anything. The tortuous climb from newspaper features to literary essays, from the tight short story to the expansive novel, from poetic translation to the travel book has demanded submitting oneself to the demanding discipline of each aspect of the craft. And at each curve of the uphill road, when I have looked up and seen the still faraway peak, the edge of my despair has been softened by the masters of each genre, their struggles, their methods and their achievements. Besides the ones already named in this essay, you will find many others between these covers, each an inspiration in his own way – Michael Ondaatje and Che Guevara, Truman Capote and John Steinbeck, Joseph Conrad and Anton Chekhov. This collection of *Second Thoughts* is my tribute to these great masters.

Journals of the Footloose

Immobilized by the heat outside, in which only the blushing bougainvillea could dare to sway gently, I spent the weekend among the travellers on my bookshelf. And imperceptibly, the yearning to be footloose again crept upon me. To watch the stars from a train rushing at night across a desert, to wait impatiently for the dawn to break over some pale, rose-pink mountain, to meet a stranger in a café and strike up a conversation that would open up a new world. And, as in the past, write it all down in a wire-bound journal, desperately trying to capture every inflection, every nuance, every shade. Damascus, Istanbul, the Baltic shore, the blues singers of Memphis, a familiar voice in Berlin, two old ladies on a Sunday bus in New York, Auschwitz on a haunted afternoon … But now these memories are tinged by a niggling doubt: has the eye jaded, will the journals ever be filled again? For reassurance, through vicarious experience, I turned to the footloose on my bookshelf.

They step down proudly, stylists all, with their windcheaters and rucksacks and trekking shoes. The scholar sits easily with the humorist, the sharp eye gives a crucial edge to lyricism, the pungent jibe is softened with sudden sympathy. There is the doyen, the ninety-one-year-old Patrick Leigh Fermor, who walked from Rotterdam to Istanbul, reciting poetry aloud, when not yet twenty. Casting himself in the Byronic mould, and like T.E. Lawrence not satisfied by simply being an aesthete, he lived a life of action, including meeting affable highwaymen in Hungarian forests and helping to capture a Nazi general for the Crete resistance. Fermor started writing about his long trek forty years later and likened it to reconstructing a brontosaurus from half an eye socket and a basket full of bones. Recalling far-off memories is obviously difficult; hence my passion for wire-bound journals.

The blue-eyed Bruce Chatwin stares handsomely from the dust jacket of *In Patagonia*. When temporarily blinded by too much staring at impressionist art as part of his work at Sotheby's, he was advised to look at horizons. He needed no further goading and was off to Africa, the Middle East, and Central Asia, recording his impressions in chiselled prose. That there was fiction instilled into fact, as in *The Songlines*, may have disappointed fans but seems to have not bothered him overly.

Eric Newby jostles for attention. To read *The Big Red Train Ride in Moscow* was to be forever obsessed with the desire to board the Trans Siberian express, a desire that will remain unfulfilled for the Soviet version of that train is now one with the past. But he taught me that a squash ball is a useful water stopper in old Soviet-style hotels. And

meet Pico Iyer, that lyrical poet of the lonely places, whose *Falling off the Map* deserves to be read many times. And Paul Theroux, whose one ghost story has haunted me on every trip through South-east Asia, whenever palm trees have bent under coastal rain and lamps have burned low in white houses with red-tiled roofs. And Peter Hopkirk, Peter Fleming, Jack Kerouac ...

But the one that I stay with most of the weekend is Robert Byron, also cast in the mould of his namesake, describing himself as being 'of melancholy appearance' in his passport form. Drawn inexorably by a photograph of an eleventh century Persian funerary tower, he travelled across Persia and Afghanistan to produce *The Road to Oxiana*, which, it has been said, is to travel writing what *Ulysses* is to the novel or *The Wasteland* to poetry. Chatwin called it 'a sacred text, and thus beyond criticism' and carried his 'spineless and flood-stained' copy as he slavishly followed Byron's footsteps through four journeys in Central Asia.

Byron called travel a 'spiritual necessity' and believed
that the 'traveller is slave to his senses, his grasp of fact can
only be completed when reinforced by sensory evidence;
he can know the world, in fact, only when he sees, hears
and smells it.' Whether it is Tehran or Isfahan, Herat or
Kabul, Byron brings it all alive. The soft dawns and the
liquid violet-blue skies, the sweet melons and grapes and
the sudden sight of a tangerine tree in an inner courtyard,
picnics on carpets thrown casually alongside mountain
streams, 'the unearthly treble' of the muezzin's call, the
shimmering beauty of turquoise leek-shaped domes, the
snow cone of Mt Demavand and the landscape around
'where mountains rippled up and sighed away like the
wash of a tide ...'

I too have walked the streets of Tehran at dawn and
watched the chinar leaves float gently into bubbling water
channels. I have stood in the high verandah of the Ali
Qappu palace in Isfahan and watched entranced the play
of form, pattern and colour of the Sheikh Lutfullah mosque
across the massive maidan. I have sat and sipped black tea
under the arch of a bridge on the lazy Zayendeh rud not far
away. And Byron's descriptions are only a reconfirmation.

Byron's talent for architectural observation and lyrical
prose are equally evident in the 1931 special issue of *The
Architectural Review* devoted to New Delhi, a month before
the capital's official opening. To read his descriptions is to
find new secrets in the familiar creations of Lutyens and the
somewhat neglected Baker. Emerging from old Delhi, he

sees rising on one side of a plain littered with the remains of former empires, 'a scape of towers and domes ... lifted from the horizon, sunlit pink and cream against the dancing blue sky, fresh as a cup of milk, grand as Rome'. The dome of Rashtrapati Bhavan 'seems not to have been built, but to have been poured compact from a mould, impermeable to age, destined to stand forever, to watch the rise of an eighth Delhi and a hundredth Delhi'. One may no longer be able to see the Qutub—'an extravagant chimney on the south horizon'—from atop South Block. But a Delhi evening can still be as beautiful as then described: 'Dusk approached, falling like a curtain. The lights come out, furlongs of gold dots, suffusing the sky with an electric blue that deepens to black. Stars complete the night, a powder of silver.' Yes, he is the best among them, king of the travellers on my bookshelf.

'I Remember You Well in Chelsea Hotel'

Just back from a quick trip to the Himachal hills, a news snippet about the reclusive poet and singer Leonard Cohen catches the eye. He has made a rare appearance in Toronto to promote his first book in twenty-two years and to make some money after being allegedly duped by his manager of about five million dollars. To me that does not mean much; a few million dollars here or there matter to those who have them.

It's the connection between Cohen and the hills that is important. There, as I discovered thirty-five years ago, he is something else. He reached out to our young hearts from an old tape played out on a small cassette player tied to the belt, the great-grandparent of the iPod. His magic was magnified and his words skimmed our souls as we climbed up to Jalori pass, or struggled across alpine flower-decked meadows of Chandrakhani pass, or slithered down the steep descent to Malana. And as we bathed at sunset in the little stream rushing to meet the Sutlej at Ani or toasted our tired limbs in the hot springs at Manikaran, his ballads revealed hidden depths.

Those were the days of adventure and heartbreak, of unknown restless futures and half-hidden promises. Disappointments were rare, while victories were only to be expected. Cohen's moody baritone met all these moods; he could pluck at our heartstrings with '*That's no way to say goodbye*'; he could conjure up visions with '*Suzanne*'; he could send us hastening across the hills with '*So long, Marianne*'.

Thirty years on, neither the hills nor Cohen have lost their magic. Just the other day, I landed up at a friend's cottage in the relative wild at two in the morning. The hillside and the valleys below lay bathed in the lambent light of the Buddha Purnima moon. Once again, there was restlessness in the step, life's moorings seemed to have been loosened, a certain disconsolation had entered the heart, reality and unreality mingled in resigned sadness. As he opened the door and we watched the moonlight spread across the night, I said: 'Don't turn on the light, you can read their address by the moon.' He quietly nodded: 'Sisters of Mercy.' There was no need for more words. We had both long ago listened to Cohen in the hills.

As I muse on the news cutting, I wonder if Cohen will go down to New York City to promote his book and if he does, will he again stay at Chelsea Hotel, as he has so many times in the past. His whimsical verse comes to mind:

> I don't mean to suggest that I loved you the best
> I can't keep track of each fallen robin
> I remember you well in Chelsea Hotel
> That's all, I don't even think of you that often.

That was written for one-time lover and fellow resident of Chelsea, Janis Joplin, after the twenty-seven-year-old rock and roll sensation died from a heroin overdose. He began writing it in a bar in Miami and finished it in Ethiopia just before the coup, not in the hotel it commemorates.

That song drumming in my mind, I sought out Chelsea Hotel on 23rd Street, deep on the west side of New York one windy evening. Far away from the skyscrapers and nearer to the more randomly laid out Greenwich Village, it was difficult to believe that this red brick building was once the tallest in the city. But that was way back in 1884.

Its height is not its claim to fame but rather the fact that besides Cohen and Joplin, scores of other writers, artists, poets have stayed and worked in its rooms. The names, many of them marked by commemorative plaques at the entrance, make fascinating reading.

Mark Twain and Tennessee Williams lived here. Thomas Wolfe wrote *Look Homeward, Angel* here. And then came the beatniks of the 1950s, the hippies of the 1960s and the rock 'n rollers of the 1970s. Arthur Miller, famous playwright and one-time husband of Marilyn Monroe, stayed and worked here for six years. The Welsh poet, Dylan Thomas, sailed forth from this hotel to the White Horse tavern in the village and died in a coma after eighteen straight whiskies. The man whom he gave a name to—Bob Dylan—lived, sang and even had a child here. Arthur C. Clarke wrote his famous *2001* here and was often visited by Kubrick during the making of the film. The list goes on ...

Jimi Hendrix, O. Henry, Vladimir Nabakov, Edith Piaf, Henri Cartier Bresson, Jane Fonda, Andy Warhol, Jackson Pollock ... Short stories, novels, plays, songs, paintings have been produced in this ten-storey building with its slow elevators, narrow corridors, decadent carpets.

As I stood in silent homage in its lobby that looked like an art gallery, the place seemed to spell artistic achievement and hinted constantly at destructive tragedy. Nonchalance and art were everywhere, style seemed to be leaning at the porch. One could understand what Miller meant when he wrote: 'I witnessed how a new time, the sixties, stumbled into the Chelsea with young, bloodshot eyes.'

And if Cohen does go there, far from my hills where I love to listen to him, he may recall that it was the kind of hotel where 'at four a.m. you can bring along a midget, a bear and four ladies, drag them to your room and no one cares about it at all'.

Of Roses and Poets

Twenty some years ago, a friendly captain of an Air India jumbo invited me into the cockpit during a flight back from Paris. It was a magical clear night and we were somewhere over the waters. My eyes searched the skies for the moon and the stars. On my left appeared the dark solidity of land and then a distant constellation of lights. 'That's Shiraz, in Iran,' the captain said. The night flight passed but that magical name, redolent with wine and reminiscent of immortal poetry, stayed on in the consciousness till a drizzly spring day many years later, when I landed in the city of roses and poets in the Fars province of Iran, the province that gives the name Farsi to the language.

Shiraz, lying in the foothills of the Zagros mountains, spells fantasy for many reasons: its gardens and orangeries, magnificent cypress trees, pear-shaped turquoise-domed mosques, the origin of winemaking, the name of the grape, and so on. But what tugs at the heart is that there is no other city with a name so synonymous with poetry, for there is no other city that is the home and resting place of the two great poets, Saadi and Hafiz.

That drizzly day happens to be Nowroz, the Persian New Year, celebrated enthusiastically in Islamic Iran. The roads all seem to lead to the tombs of the two poets; the crowds, including many newly-wed couples, carrying picnic baskets with naan, cottage cheese and watermelons, are obviously on a pilgrimage. I follow, overwhelmed at this unusual subjugation of all else to the gods of poetry.

Saadi, who died in 1291 at the age of 100, rests in a pleasant garden with a natural spring and a fishpond. People crowd around his grave, gently placing two fingers on the stone above the poet's head, reverently reading the inscriptions on the walls of the canopy. It seems to be a well-deserved rest for an indefatigable traveller who visited Arabia, India, Egypt, Syria, Afghanistan … staying as long as he fancied. He was captured by Franks, sold to Jews, ransomed for ten dinars in Allepo and married off to his rescuer's daughter. But evidently she could not hold him and he returned to

Shiraz to tell his inimitable stories of places and people in his two main works, *Gulistan* and *Bustan*. Inscribed over his tomb is what he desired: 'From the tomb of Saadi, son of Shiraz—the perfume of love escapes—Thou shall smell it still a thousand years after his death.'

We are past 800, and it still does.

Not far away, in another garden with a less formal setting, under tall cypress trees, lies Hafiz, heir to Rumi and Saadi. But for one move to Isfahan and Yazd, Hafiz spent his entire life in Shiraz, writing under spiritual inspiration but using romantic allegories of wine, drunkenness and human love to produce ghazals of incredible spontaneity and rich musical quality. Anecdotes about the poet's life abound: Hafiz means one who knows the Koran by heart and, as a child, he had learnt it thus from his father's recitations. His father died early and the young Hafiz began to work in a bakery to help his mother out of debt. While delivering bread, he fell helplessly in love with a very beautiful Turkish woman, Shakh-e-Nabat (literally branch of sugarcane), and the poems that he wrote in love for her made him famous. My rough translation of the best-known one is:

> If that Turkish beauty of Shiraz, holds my heart in her hand
> For the mole on her cheek, I will sacrifice Samarkand and Bukhara

Hafiz's generosity in sacrificing Samarkand and Bukhara was questioned, according to some biographies, by none

other than Timur, when he occupied Shiraz towards the
end of the fourteenth century. How dare you, asked the
invader, hand over my beloved cities for the mole on the
cheek of some girl? Hafiz, pointing to his poor attire, is said
to have replied: 'It is because of such prodigality that I live in
such poverty.' Timur's anger ebbed and Hafiz walked away
with rich gifts. Timur, incidentally and contrary to popular
image, seems to have had an intellectual bent of mind. He
is also known to have had a six-week discourse outside the
walls of a besieged Damascus with the Islamic historian
Ibn Khaldun on all manner of issues of the day. Khaldun
later described him as 'highly intelligent and perspicacious,
addicted to debate and argumentation about what he
knows and also about what he does not know.'

But back to the master of the ghazal, lying now under
an octagonal cupola, whose popularity long ago crossed
over to reverence. In most Iranian houses, a divan of
Hafiz can be found along with the Koran. Iranians often
use it to seek *faal* or oracular divination, opening a page at
random and seeking guidance from the verse that emerges.
A souvenir shop in one corner of this garden does a brisk
sale of beautiful illustrated versions of the divan. His
admirers crave no greater benediction than being able to
read his poems in the proximity of his grave. To them, one
verse from the ghazal inscribed on his tomb is an eternal
invitation: *Sit near my tomb, and bring wine and music—
Feeling thy presence I shall come out of my sepulchre—Rise,
softly moving creature, and let me contemplate thy beauty.*

Across the courtyard from the grave is a charming traditional teahouse, complete with rug-covered wooden beds, hubble-bubbles, and orange trees around a small pool. A dervish emerges from the teahouse, his layered hat resembling the cupola over Hafiz. Gently and with measured steps, he walks past the grave of a man who called himself 'the only dervish in the world who can't dance'.

A Daiquiri, Then a Mojito

The sun takes its time setting over Havana. It lingers, as if unable to leave this city of a certain unreal charm. And when it does finally sink across the blue silver water that stretches to the western horizon, it leaves a telltale point of departure which continues to impart an orange-pink fringe to the low-lying range of clouds.

Shades of the same orange-pink are splashed randomly across the sky, casual farewell strokes by some truly talented artist. As the water changes shades, from a light silvery blue to a serious steel, a group of joyous teenagers who have been jumping repeatedly into the water turn into thoughtful silhouettes, sobered by the celestial play of day turning into night, gradually.

Reluctantly I turn away. A hundred invitations seem to step out of the twilight shadows. A walk along the Malecon, past the entwined couples and the beer drinkers, eyes on the dark ocean, the wind in my face. Surely it would be like so many evenings on the Marine Drive wall, moody and intense, or like a late-night bridge below the Eiffel where conversations ended only to start again and the metro trains crossed over our shoulders in the Parisian night.

Or I could wander along the narrow, sloping cobbled streets of old Havana, weave in and out of its colonnaded corridors, step into sudden serendipitous squares, listen to the jazz band playing on the stoop across the broad-shouldered cathedral, peep into art galleries, private courtyards and mysterious half-open doorways sibilant with whispering possibilities.

Or I could sit in one of the open-air restaurants, listening to the music from the laughing Cuban band and engage in convoluted conversations that may help me understand the complexities of Castro's Cuba ...

But there are other trysts to be kept, a literary pilgrimage to be made. It begins at the El Floridita, an art deco bar and restaurant in old Havana that loudly proclaims itself to be the cradle of the daiquiri.

Ernest Hemingway stayed often at the Hotel Ambos Mundos in the 1930s and was a regular at El Floridita. His full-size statue leans heavily in one corner, its shoulder worn smooth from the number of people who daringly put an arm around Papa for the ritual photograph. The daiquiris are chilled and smooth and it is good to be in that wood-panelled room and peer at the black-and-white photographs, including one of Hemingway and Fidel.

But this is not the only bar he haunted. There is also the La Bodeguita Del Medio, which is smaller, cosier and more musical. It makes its living on the basis of a signed Hemingway certificate: 'My daiquiri at Floridita, my mojito at Bodeguita.' The mojitos are made—and drunk—hand

over fist and as a glass is jostled, a young woman catches the drops in mid-flight and dabs them, like a precious perfume, in the hollow of her neck.

Partly to keep him away from these bars and partly to get away from a hotel room, Hemingway's third wife Martha Gellhorn—Scott Fitzgerald had predicted that Ernest would probably need a new wife for each book—followed up a newspaper advertisement and found Finca Vigia, a fifteen-acre quiet farm a few miles out of Havana.

Hemingway did not like what he first saw of the dilapidated colonial house but while he went on a fishing trip, Martha paid up the rent—$100 a month—and the deed was done. He did obviously take to it thereafter and bought it with the money that *For Whom the Bells Toll* brought him.

It was left to his fourth wife Mary Welsh to convert Finca Vigia into a comfortable home ... fruit and vegetable gardens, a well-lit library, a workroom, a sprawling living-room, a swimming pool, a tennis court and a bungalow for his sons and guests.

Today his fishing boat *El Pillar* that he used for marlin fishing in the Gulf Stream and even fitted with machine guns to hunt German U-boats during the war is on display on the tennis court.

The graves of his four favourite dogs recall the menagerie that Finca Vigia, with its sixty cats, must have once been. Mary added a tower that had a room with his desk, bookcase, bearskin and large windows with views of Havana where she wanted him to write. He, however, preferred to write standing up early in the morning, on his typewriter placed on a bookshelf in the workroom of the main house.

Besides finishing *For Whom the Bells Toll*, Hemingway wrote several books here, including *Across the River and into the Trees* and, most famously, *The Old Man and the Sea*—the story of a Cuban fisherman's struggle with a big fish.

It brought him the Nobel prize and he insisted, as the Cubans fondly recall, that when Hollywood make a film, they should include the ordinary people from Cojimar, the little Cuban fishing village that forms the novel's backdrop.

His other passion seems to have been keeping a watch on his weight: nearly fifteen years of records are scribbled in pencil on the bathroom wall!

After Hemingway committed suicide, Mary carried away about 200 pounds of paper and burnt much more, donating the property to the Cuban people. What remain in the museum are 9,000 books and magazines—including a termite-invaded copy of *For Whom the Bells Toll*.

Also on view are his shoes, his war correspondent's jacket (in surprisingly good condition) and the heads of the big game that he hunted, including the giant kudu for which, the story goes, Mussolini sent Hemingway a blank cheque. The latter returned it with the advice that if Mussolini wanted a kudu, he should go to Africa and hunt one.

As I step into the dappled sunshine on the sloping drive, birds rise from the surrounding palms. And it is easy to imagine how the Finca was home even to as restless a soul as Hemingway.

Your Mumbai, My Bombay

I have just put aside *Sacred Games*, Vikram Chandra's mammoth new novel. I kept imagining Chandra standing on the crumbling sea wall of Marine Drive, swinging a fisherman's net over his head. Then, at the last moment, with the net in full vicious swing, he releases it not over the sea but towards the salt-corroded buildings behind him. The net swings over those buildings, over suburban stations, maidans, slums, Bollywood ... And when he skilfully draws it in, the catch is thrashing, violent, disturbing, mean ... everything except beautiful. It consists of all that is at the base of the human soul—treachery, deceit, unbridled ambition, murder, mayhem ... That is a Mumbai I can accept, but cannot like. The disturbing images continue to flash in the eyes long after the book has been kept away. I need to get away from them; I need to think again of the beauty of Bombay.

... Of the first monsoon that I saw there years ago, when the lanes of Fort Bombay used to be a sea of black umbrellas and we rushed somehow to the best Irani restaurant that we knew in those days. Not so much for the fare it offered but for the pretty face of the owner's daughter, who stood at the counter and watched us with languorous distant grace. And then we walked back to our offices dodging those black umbrellas, past stands selling mint chutney-tomato-cucumber sandwiches, belts, handkerchiefs, locks, sunglasses ... I bought more airmail envelopes there than one could ever use in a lifetime. I bought them because their blue-and-red edges spelt romance, distant shores, adventures in lands I may never see. And past the inevitable pavement booksellers outside the old post office, the eye keenly looking for a forgotten title, a rare edition ...

... Of hunting desperately for paying guest accommodation in huge buildings—Queen's Court, Green Fields, Moonlight, Sunshine, Framroze Court ... and being interviewed by old elegant Parsi ladies in well-appointed drawing rooms with clusters of silver-framed photographs of weddings, dogs, horses ... And the joy of finally finding a room with a view where the carpet matched the curtains. The bath had hot water, the tea never enough sugar but there were always mangoes with breakfast. From the

shelter of the balcony I watched the tide come in at night, heaving and dark, pulled in by a whimsical moon. The swish of the water grew even stronger and the sigh as it hit the rocks would waft up in the night air as I leaned out and watched Victoria carriages trotting up and down Marine Drive, the hooves of the horses echoing sharply. There was the smell of jasmine in the air, the generous sea breeze fresh despite its pungent sting, the call of the peanut-seller, an occasional peal of laughter that electrified the night. In the early morning, the scene from the balcony would be very different—the sea held no dark secrets, the water had receded to reveal large rocks, the romantic couples of the night before were replaced by joggers, ships waiting to berth dotted the horizon, the dark torso of a fisherman on a lone boat bent, pulled, rose ...

.... Of a lake in Powai. And a lingering evening of ineluctable magic, with the lengthening shadows of the trees winning over the last touch of the light of the setting sun and the wide-bodied planes coming up over the lake, their wheels going up, gaining height, taking people further away, their lights saying farewell and, suddenly, the lazy singing of Hemant Kumar across the grounds, tugging at emotions that lie in the crevices of the soul, hiding from hurt ...

... Of late-night journeys in suburban trains that were once the symbol of safety and civility of a city. Watching tired foursomes play rummy on briefcases balanced on their knees, while the stations swept by, their verandahs taken over by sleeping urchins, beggars, boot-polish boys, the red light still revolving in the weighing machines, raucous night laughter spreading in circles from the paan stalls. Those nights had a freedom of their own; no one cared much about anything. There was an anonymity that was precious, an indifference that did not hurt. The same anonymity that one felt in the morning rush hour and yet there was a strange bonding for, more often than not, one crossed the same face at the same place day after day.

... Of sitting on Chowpatty beach on Ganesh Chaturthi, watching the idols, big, bigger and biggest, arriving on shoulders, carriages, trucks, and being slowly pushed into the moonlit waters, and wafting away towards unknown dark shores or down to the mysterious deep, accompanied by the mesmerising chants of *Ganapati Bapa Maurya* ...

... And there are many other memories ... memories of a sea that sparkles with the magical iridescence of a thousand stars when the sun comes up, of long evening walks to sit in silence on the sea wall, of breakfasts in an Irani restaurant that can never ever be repeated, of chilled beer on a very hot afternoon ... and many more which should perhaps never be written out, lest their fragile beauty tarnish, lest they lose the haunting ache that they enclose ...

So Vikram, you keep your gritty Mumbai and I will keep my lost Bombay and let's just let it be.

Landscapes of the Mind

This large glass window looks on to a peak the villagers call Shali. The early morning light caresses the valleys, skims the tops of the deodars and glints off the white walls of the temple that sits atop the peak. Not far beyond the spur on my left lies Mashobra with its sinuous bazaar, its shops under constant threat from the well-fed monkeys. There is little else to hold the mind or the eye, just the mountain ranges that stretch out in the light blue distance, enveloping their chessboards of light and shadow, aloof in their silences, absorbed in meditation. The old question about a writing landscape arises again. Are the silences enough to constantly feed the mind? Can one narrow bazaar yield enough stories if only one knows how to look for them? Or does one need to be in the midst of it all, rubbing shoulders with characters, living out the adventures, being part of the stories?

Orhan Pamuk, the flavour of that literary season because of his recent Nobel that year, sheds some light. Somewhere he has answered the same question, saying that as long as he can see Istanbul with all its sounds and smells, it is enough for him, for it is that city that has made him. Pamuk has many other companions in writers who have used a familiar enclosed landscape for their fiction—Malgudi for R.K. Narayan, Yoknapatawpha county for William Faulkner and his not-so-fictional Mussoorie for Ruskin Bond—in contrast to the more footloose authors who have travelled far and become part of the worlds that they have written about—Joseph Conrad, V.S. Naipaul, Ernest Hemingway, Paul Theroux ...

Pamuk's Istanbul must be read, not only because of his entry into the Nobel league, but because Istanbul is a world of its own. There are few cities like that—only Damascus and Isfahan come to mind—where everything seems possible, where entire worlds submerge into a crowded lane. Even a fleeting brush with such a city can mark one forever, leave images that can linger in the mind for years, evoke yearnings that tug constantly ...

... Standing on the deck of a boat at night, going up and down the Bosphorus, floating past minarets and palaces, Asia on one side, Europe on the other. The darkest romance,

the deepest contradictions, the sharpest conflict could occur in such a landscape. Every time the boat goes under one of the huge bridges, the two continents seem to connect, clash, merge, and all conversation becomes meaningless; the glass of wine lies on the deck table, untouched.

... Or sitting in the gardens on the Asian side, wondering how people go to work every day from here to there. The night redolent with flowers, the boat now floating away, towards the darkness of the harbour. I hear the story of pollution, crowds, economic difficulty, but nothing seems to detract from the romance.

... Wandering through the huge courtyard of the Blue Mosque, with its six minarets. There is a quiet and simplicity here that defines the purity of worship and calms the mind. The scale brings to mind the courtyard of the Omayyad mosque in Damascus, the historical seat of the Caliphs, where the head of St John the Baptist lies buried.

... Or gasping at the huge, apparently weightless dome of the Hagia Sophia, the unique structure which has served both as church and mosque. Civilizations merge, religions coalesce at this crossroads of history.

Pamuk's Nobel will perhaps repay some of his debt to the city by bringing it to the front rows of bookshelves and to the glass window displays of bookshops. But then, every writer does not get the Nobel and the list of those who have not tells its own story about literary prizes. In fact the Nobel Prize for literature started with controversy in its very first year when the committee chose someone called Rene

Sully-Prudhomme over Leo Tolstoy. It continued to court criticism by inexplicably ignoring such master craftsmen as Thomas Hardy, Marcel Proust, Emile Zola, James Joyce (a committee member is said to have asked, 'Joyce? Who's he?'), Franz Kafka, Virginia Woolf, Mark Twain, Henrik Ibsen, Chekhov ... and got to George Bernard Shaw only at the age of sixty-nine. Shaw told the judges that the money was like throwing a lifebelt to a swimmer who had already reached the shore in safety.

I have my own list of three favourites among the omissions, so over-the-top that they hardly ever figure even in the generally quoted omission lists. F. Scott Fitzgerald, the author of *The Great Gatsby*, often listed as the top novel of the last century, got nowhere near the prize. Was it his alcoholism, or his celebration of the lifestyles of the rich and famous, that put off the judges? And Graham Greene who, in book after book, clinically unveiled the human soul. Was it his cynical, baleful gaze that pierced the human condition, his leaving the church, his relentless examination of deceit, adultery, betrayal that denied him this recognition? And why is it that P.G. Wodehouse, 'the performing flea of English literature', is never even vaguely mentioned as a possibility? Was it that innocent mistake of the radio interviews for Nazi Germany? Else, how can one keep out of any list the man who is said to have made the English language jump through hoops and created an entire world that has delighted readers for a hundred years—unless, of course, he was considered too light in humourless Stockholm.

Give Me Your Seconds

In the 1960s, Dehra Dun's Paltan Bazaar was as throbbing a slice of life as one could wish for. Cycling downhill from the clock tower, a schoolboy could weave nonchalantly through the crowd, past shops selling imitation Bata shoes, Tip-Top cold drinks, school uniforms and everything else that the most demanding household could possibly need. Dark brown, delicious gulab jamuns floated in gargantuan containers, crisp aloo tikkis were fried at the corner, peanuts and chikki sold in the light of paraffin lamps, a row of paan shops provided convenient mirrors for young men to comb their hair in the latest Shashi Kapoor, Dharmendra, Biswajeet style and an appetising fragrance of freshly baked bread added the magic. Enchanting, but not exactly the kind of place where one would expect to find an education in classical English Literature.

But, one day, this schoolboy took a by-lane. Cycling past a row of ladies' tailors, he reached some wooden shacks selling school notebooks, HB pencils, scented erasers and the now-extinct Sulekha ink. In one of these sat a genial old man, his visage amazingly like P.G. Wodehouse, his smile hiding delightful secrets. He pushed aside a curtain and showed me what was to prove to be my key to literature: a huge bundle of Classics Illustrated—I somehow cannot make myself call them comics. Initially only four were purchased, for four annas each. And then a generous father stepped in, himself bitten by the bug. The classics began to gather—*Silas Marner, Julius Ceaser, Cleopatra, Twenty Thousand Leagues under the Sea* ... until everything that the Wodehouse look-alike could procure was bought and handed over to another one of the wooden stores, to be bound in batches of four. I have little embarrassment in admitting that so deep was the impact of those fine images that one never felt the need to read many of the books in full. What could match the poignant visage of Sydney Carton on the last page, as he looked up at the sky and said, 'It is a far, far better thing that I do, than I have ever done' or the anguish of Caesar as he looked over his shoulder and muttered, 'Yon Cassius has a lean and hungry look' or the heartbreak of Cyrano de Bergerac reciting poetry below his cousin's balcony.

Paltan Bazaar is now a horribly crowded alley, my smiling benefactor has passed on, and his wooden shack has gone the way of much else that belonged to a lost world, but those volumes of second-hand Classics Illustrated with their spines of red cloth lie as a family treasure, to be read by the young of another generation in the curtained rooms of the summers of their youth.

Since then I have never resisted the charm of any shop that sells second-hand books, a charm distilled from an alchemy of the ageless smell of yellowing pages, the tenderness of an inscription to a loved one on the fly leaf, a trenchant comment pencilled in the margin. Added to that is the uniqueness of the experience—of knowing that one will meet neither revolving shelves containing the selection of the week nor authors organized in alphabetical order. Just about anything may be tucked in anywhere; it is all in the luck of the draw. And once the deed is done, nobody else will get the book with that angled handwriting of the first owner, or that decades-old forgotten bookmark, or sometimes even a stranger's photograph.

From Paltan Bazaar to Paris. Hoofing around the city in the fall of 1983, I rummaged through some cartons full of old books outside a shop and came out victorious with Scribner versions of *Tender Is the Night* and *This Side of Paradise* with their broad pages, comfortable font, and that cover which is neither paperback nor hardback. The cartons had been put outside by George Whitman, another aging, kindly soul who set up the world famous bookshop 'Shakespeare and Co.' in 1951 on the left bank of the Seine. I have since wandered through that shop on every visit to Paris—even during a six-hour transit halt on a drizzly afternoon—searching up and down its three floors crammed with books, through cubby-hole rooms with rugs and comfortable chairs, and a bed in which many a struggling writer has spent a night free of charge, right up to a kitchen where one can make coffee. Be not inhospitable to strangers, Whitman believes, lest they be angels in disguise. And one should believe that all the more of struggling writers.

As many bookshops as there have been cities, and the evidence is scattered at random on the bookshelves. A burgundy leather copy of *Self Help* by Samuel Smiles, received in Dharamsala, *Punjab* by a certain Robert Percy Thatcher, published in November 1895 and picked up in a little shop in the hills. A hardcover copy of *The Essential Hemingway* brings to mind a big hall in an unlikely building in Fort, Bombay. A Wodehouse in Italian was pocketed for a rupee on a chaotic pavement outside the old GPO at Flora Fountain. A marvellous leather-bound copy of Keats that somebody bought in Valparaiso, wherever that is, came to hand in Bookworm, a haven for the lover of English books in francophone Geneva. A picture of Keats's grave is pasted in the book, with the epigraph, written by the poet himself on his deathbed, 'Here lies one whose name was writ in water.'

Bookworm, which one reached after negotiating streets where mini-skirted ladies of the night stood smoking at corners, haggard and drawn in the morning light, always yielded some treasure, including my best copy of *Three Men in a Boat* and a leather-bound Shakespeare, gifted by one friend to another in memory of a happy birthday spent together in 1936. Two more Scribner Fitzgeralds— *The Beautiful and the Damned* and *The Last Tycoon* have drifted in from Blossom in Bangalore to give company to their Parisian sisters.

An old sketch of Persepolis recalls the treasure trove that was Second Story in downtown Washington D.C. D.H. Lawrence's *The Complete Short Stories* will remind me forever of a wintry windy day in the old square of The Hague. And the excitement of a first visit to Islamabad reached fever pitch when I found the shop that yielded so many photographs of nineteenth-century Lahore and a wealth of old Hemingways and Joseph Conrads. But the last time I was there, the shopkeeper said, somewhat sheepishly, 'Your books are now upstairs, sir.' And there they were, a mere shelf load; the rest of the shop was full of new books, bic pens, and school tiffin boxes.

Why are all good things doomed to go away?

Water, Stone and Sky

The Gulf of Finland is a choppy grey this afternoon. Two long low hydrofoils waft uncomfortably in the water. The strong breeze blows in a sharp drizzle from the sea. A sea gull squawks hoarsely as it drops suddenly to the heaving waves. A grey endlessness, broken only by a lone lighthouse, stretches to that hint of a horizon, where a grey sky lingers uncertainly on the sea. It is a starkly bleak scene, and it is beautiful. A similar scene may well have greeted Peter the Great, when he rode up to this edge of Russian earth in 1703, looking for a place to build a fortress to contain the Swedes. Something in that misty landscape must have touched his heart, for he cut two strips of peat with his bayonet and, laying them on the ground in a cross, determined: Here shall be a town.

And what a town then rose from the marshy overgrown network of islands. Millions of conscripts and serfs laboured day and night for five decades to create St Petersburg, a symphony in stone, played out against a backdrop of river and sea. The granite monolith on which the equestrian statue of Peter the Great, symbol of the city, today stands, perhaps best manifests the scale of the effort. Weighing more than six hundred thousand kilos, the granite was moved from the forest clearing where it was found to its present position, 13 km away, by a thousand men over a period of eighteen months. Peter's bronze horse is poised in mid-air, and it is difficult to say whether it is rearing back from what it sees ahead, or raring to go forward. Pushkin immortalized this statue in his epic poem 'The Bronze Horseman', making it emblematic of Russian destiny.

On a shore by the desolate waves
He stood, with lofty thoughts.
And gazed into the distance ...

It was not just a city that Peter built; he made a powerful civilizational statement. Russia was also Europe. She needed to be westernized; she needed to break away from the confines of archaic, medieval Muscovy. St Petersburg was the door through which Russia would pass and become European. It was to represent all that was modern, progressive, Western, enlightened. Its grace would match that of Paris, its baroque ornate architecture would rival that of Rome, its blending of stone and water would suggest Venice. Its imperial formality contrasted sharply with a dishevelled, rough-and-ready Moscow, which was the beating heart of traditional Russia—warm, friendly, informal, hedonistic, but culturally insular. Gogol's comparison of the two cities is eloquent: 'Petersburg is an accurate, punctual kind of person, a perfect German, and he looks at everything in a calculated way. Before he gives a party he will look into his accounts. Moscow is a Russian nobleman, and if he's going to have a good time, he'll go all the way until he drops, and he won't worry about how much he's got in his pocket.'

Walking by the Neva, with the Hermitage behind me, I stare through the heavy drizzle at the Peter and Paul fortress across the river, the burnished gold needle of its steeple piercing the haze. On both banks, the classical facades stretch away in artistic ensembles of avenues and squares. Palaces, winter and summer, large and small, noblemen's houses, hospitals and barracks, built by architects for whom space was suddenly no concern. Bound only by their own imaginations, they had eagerly set to work on the empty vastness that stretched before them like an inviting canvas.

The city did not grow, as cities do, but seemed to come out of the water like a miracle, a fantastical apparition in a bubble that might vanish at the slightest touch. Legends cloaked its birth— Peter's ghost was often seen walking the streets, mythical beasts flew over churches; floods were curses coming to claim what had always belonged to the water.

But while it lasted, it flourished. In its eighteenth century salons, behind those tall windows, gentle conversations took place in French and soft-spoken gentlemen danced European waltzes with blushing debutantes. These were generations who would rather have been European than Russian, the 'superfluous men' whose descendants would people nineteenth century Russian literature—Pushkin's Eugene Onegin, Lermontov's Pechorin and Turgenev's Rudin. 1812 and Napolean changed all that. A deep desire to go back to things Russian—way of life, language, arts, cuisine—came to the fore. The Russian spirit entered Petersburg too. Behind the classical facades, traditional, unruly Russian households began to multiply. French accents became a disadvantage.

The Westerniser and the Slavophile clashed; the split in the psyche was complete and needed to be healed. To the Russian nationalist, St Petersburg, with its foreign influences and manners, was a city that alienated the Russian from his true roots.

Gogol, working as a clerk during the day and writing in an attic at night, invoked this alienation to fire his prose: 'Oh have no faith in Nevsky Prospekt,' he writes of the city's most famous, grand avenue. 'It is all a deception, a dream, nothing is what it seems.' Against a ghostly and nightmarish vision of the city, he immortalized, most famously in his story 'The Overcoat', the lives of pitiful humble fellow clerks, huddled against their common foe, the northern cold, rushing to offices in an unreal light, condemned to loneliness in a world of grand but cruel illusion.

Dostoevsky, who said that all of Russian literature came from under Gogol's 'Overcoat', added the psychological dimension to the city he believed to be 'the most abstract and intentional city in the whole round world'. His characters, their emotions and perceptions unhinged, inhabit the world of mist and fog, of snow and rain, of endless grey days, of bridges with open arms, and white nights that deprive men of sleep. Here the sea can easily become the sky and palaces can seem to float on water. In such a world it is easy to dream, and think that fantasy is all.

Involuntarily, I turn up the collar of my trench coat against the arrowheads of the drizzle and walk away. And do I see it, or is it a vision: a bronze horseman is chasing a poor clerk across a mighty bridge, while worn-out overcoats sway in the sky.

Monumental Searches

A small agency item, picked up from Russian TV channels, caught the eye recently. 'Unknown vandals,' it read, 'have desecrated the grave of dissident Russian poet Boris Pasternak whose novel *Doctor Zhivago* won him the Nobel Prize for literature ... The modest tombstone, at a cemetery in the famed writers' retreat of Peredelkino outside Moscow, was covered in soot as the vandals put wreaths around it and set them on fire last night ...'

Inevitably, my thoughts went back to a windy and overcast Easter day, many years ago, when we headed for Peredelkino, 25 miles south-west of Moscow. The snow had not yet melted fully and our shoulders hunched involuntarily under our coats as we searched conspiratorially around the dacha village for Pasternak's grave. In the Soviet Union of those days—as indeed today, according to the news item— he was best known as a poet, and foreigners searching for the resting place of a man known the world over as a banned novelist may well get into trouble.

It was here that Arthur Miller and his photographer wife Inge Morath had found a mad poet reciting lines from Pushkin and then got involved in an altercation when

Miller took a photograph of a security man who had been detailed to prevent them from reaching the grave.

Finally, we chanced upon a portly and elderly Russian woman who seemed safe enough to ask. 'Look for the three pines,' she smiled and walked on. Sure enough, somewhere between the birches with their peeling white trunks we found the three pines and in their shadow was the grave. Other visitors had left flowers and Easter eggs there and we stood for a while in silent contemplation before we gave in to the temptation of hot coffee and sandwiches.

That day one would never have believed that anybody could vandalize that grave. Thousands had, after all, braved official reprisal to attend Pasternak's funeral in 1960. His battle had never been with the people but rather with the Soviet state because *Doctor Zhivago* was thought to falsify the October revolution.

Calumny and pressure had ultimately forced Pasternak to refuse the Nobel and he spent his last years in his dacha, writing and gardening, a gentle man of letters who, like his Zhivago, treasured his private world.

In the words of fellow poet Yevgeny Yevtushenko, 'he went his way, leaving all the fuss to others/Firm and springy was the stride/of this silver headed artist/with a sailor's swarthy cheeks.'

But, as Trotsky had warned, the twentieth century in revolutionary Russia was not the right time for such luxuries. Somewhere the constant fear and security, the careful treading of the fine line between official acceptability

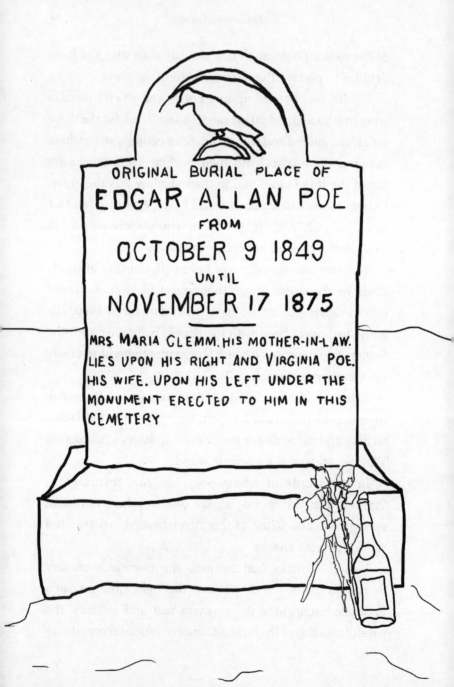

ORIGINAL BURIAL PLACE OF
EDGAR ALLAN POE
FROM
OCTOBER 9 1849
UNTIL
NOVEMBER 17 1875

MRS. MARIA CLEMM. HIS MOTHER-IN-LAW.
LIES UPON HIS RIGHT AND VIRGINIA POE.
HIS WIFE. UPON HIS LEFT UNDER THE
MONUMENT ERECTED TO HIM IN THIS
CEMETERY

and his artistic conscience must have exacted its price. For he wrote:

> Am I a gangster or a murderer?
> Of what crime do I stand
> Condemned? I made the whole world weep
> At the beauty of my land.

A pity then that a grave, which in Yevtushenko's words was to be 'a raging magnet for boys, flowers, seeds, and birds', should fall prey to vandals.

Another country, another windswept, blustery day, I searched for Graham Greene's resting place below the Swiss town of Vevey, spread out among the vineyards above a lazy Lake Leman, moodily changing its blue to grey. An article in *London Magazine* had indicated that Greene, who left Antibes and came here to be close to his daughter in his last days, was buried in the same cemetery as Charlie Chaplin, in the village of Corsier.

An hour of peering at tombstones revealed that the author of that article had obviously got it mixed up. Chaplin was there, along with wife Oona, under an impressively large headstone, but there was no sign of the enigmatic man who had made an art of exploring the frailties, ambiguities and contradictions of the human heart.

Two old ladies outside the graveyard came to the rescue. There was another small cemetery in the village of Corseaux close by, they said. The grave—number 528—was close to a nondescript side gate and there was no epitaph, only the name and the starkly written years 1904–1991.

Blue crocuses had sprouted out of the grave; a couple of rose bushes adorned its side and a grey cat watched uncertainly with its luminous eyes from behind the headstone. A fine snow began to fall and soon covered the blue of the crocuses.

And if, a few years later, it took me too long to locate Scott Fitzgerald's grave in Rockville, the mistake was entirely my own. I was searching in the sprawling Rockville cemetery where Fitzgerald had been buried in 1940 because the Baltimore diocese refused to allow him to be buried in the family plot at St Mary's Church since he had not been a devout practising Catholic.

But his daughter Scottie, supported by the Women's Club of Rockville, had managed to get the decision reversed and had her parents' remains removed to St Mary's Church. I finally found the grave behind the church, not too far from a busy traffic junction. Carved on the tombstone are the memorable last words of *The Great Gatsby*—'So we beat on, boats against the current, borne back ceaselessly into the past.'

Less than an hour away from Rockville, in the city of Baltimore, a strange ceremony takes place at the grave of Edgar Allan Poe every year on 19 January, the poet's birthday.

Since 1949, an elderly gentleman with a limp, draped in black and wearing a Fedora, a silver-tipped cane in his hand, kneels at the grave and drinks a toast of cognac. He then leaves the half-full bottle and three roses on the grave and leaves the place quietly. He is never disturbed or followed.

In recent years, observers have said that a younger man with a pretended limp has become the toaster, leading to a belief that this may be a family tradition, carried down from father to son.

The irony, as mysteriously macabre as any Poe poem, is that there is no agreement that it is indeed Poe who is buried under that impressive monument.

The Right Way to Write

The other day, faced with a blank screen for a rather long while, I could feel the creeping panic that most writers feel at some time or other. This is it, the panic seems to say, this is the end. The blank screen is going to remain blank and the sentences complete with loops and swirls are simply not going to happen. The mind then went back to several fellow travellers in the writing process whom I used to meet at the adda that Vikram Chandra would organize in an appropriately brick-lined, dimly-lit lounge on fourteenth street in Washington D.C., at the edge of the 'civilized' part of the city beyond which one was advised not to venture after dark.

The main event of the adda was the readings by the somewhat self-conscious just-published or unpublished writers leaning against the wall amidst comfortably old leather sofas and entrapped in the sophisticated decadence of red wine. But the spirit of the evening was hidden in the subtext. Most of the audience was made up of people who wanted to be writers; many had novels at various stages in their minds, or on their computers. A careful glance around the room would reveal tentative literary ambition and silent envy of the published gods. A desire to seek help with a recalcitrant manuscript usually overcame a natural tendency to shroud the pending masterpiece in secrecy. Inevitably, the writer of the evening would be asked— When do you write? Evenings? Early mornings? In long hand or on the screen? Is it autobiographical?

Sometimes the red wine would help foment more private conversations in which the writers in the making would exchange every possible idea about the writing process, searching for the secret mantra that would finally end the painful search for elusive words and result in a completed book, publication, fame. In one such weak moment I recall telling an investment-banker-during-the-day-and-budding-novelist-by-night that I could write a novel only on a computer screen and a short story only with a fountain pen, and the scratchier the nib, the more time I had to find the right nuance.

Mythology aside, the fact is that most writers tend to quickly give up faith in nebulous inspiration and are quite willing, at least amongst themselves, as at Vikram's adda, to confess to the importance of the mechanics of the writing process. That probably explains the popularity of writers groups, which go against the classic definition of the writer as recluse. These groups are made up of people who have actually paid to be amongst those who endure the same tribulation: a pitiless alchemy of blank screens, sleepless nights, unsympathetic literary agents and rejection slips. Here, ten or twelve writers in the making can unburden their soul and hope to find reassurance and perhaps the key to success. They can also, of course, pour vitriol on another's work, all in the name of constructive criticism. Most of these groups are appropriately named—Writers' Workshop, Noveldoc, Novel Advice and so on, though why anyone would like to join the group Writer's Cramp in west Seattle beats me.

Some justification for all this angst lies in the fact that even the most successful authors have put faith in some talismanic secret to please the Muse. Honore de Balzac would try and write twenty-four hours at a stretch and then take a five-hour break before starting over again. He consumed huge quantities of black coffee to beat fatigue and actually became a victim of caffeine poisoning at age fifty-one. Alexander Dumas suffered from indigestion and

the pain would wake him up in the small hours. He would then work at his writing desk till breakfast, which usually consisted of a solitary apple under the Arc de Triomphe. His poetry would be written on yellow, fiction on blue and non-fiction on rose-coloured paper. Victor Hugo would give away all his clothes to his servant with instructions that he should not return until Hugo had completed his day's work. Ben Franklin and the author of *Cyrano de Bergerac*, Edmund Rostand, preferred to work in their bathtubs. Mark Twain and R.L. Stevenson could only write when lying down and Virginia Woolf, Thomas Wolfe and Lewis Carroll had to stand up to deliver. Thomas Wolfe, at least, who confessed to finding it easier to add 75,000 words than cut down 50,000, must have been very tired on finishing *Look Homeward, Angel*. D.H. Lawrence found stimulation in climbing mulberry trees in the nude. Voltaire used his lover's back as a writing desk.

The poets, of course, had favourites of their own: Coleridge is said to have dreamt up the scene for 'Kubla Khan' under the influence of opium; Eliott would revel in writing if he had a head cold; Poe liked to have his Siamese cat on his shoulder and Schiller liked sniffing at rotten apples every once in a while.

And let's not even begin to talk of those who find the answer in alcohol. Hemingway's advice, in his classic tell-it-like-it-is style, was blunt: 'Apply the seat of the pants to the seat of the chair.' Somewhat odd though, coming from a man who is supposed to have written standing up.

Prayers Answered, Somewhat ...

An unfinished novel by a great author has all the poignancy of a bird shot in mid-flight. The same sort of questions are left, hovering hesitantly. Where exactly would the bird have melted into the twilight if it had not been shot? Would this book have been the literary tour de force that the author aspired to, a consummate culmination of his art? So it was with Scott Fitzgerald's *The Last Tycoon* and so it was with Truman Capote's *Answered Prayers*.

Capote was writing, rewriting or wanting to write *Answered Prayers*, intended to match Proust's *Remembrance of Things Past*, for more than two decades. Readers unfortunately have to make do with only three chapters bolstered by the respectability of an editor's note. When he signed the contract with Random House in 1966 with an advance of $25,000, Capote already had to his name the hugely acclaimed *Other Voices, Other Rooms*, written when he was only twenty-three, on the strength of a $15000 advance and an O. Henry short story prize. He was also the author of the immensely successful novella *Breakfast at Tiffany's*, immortalized on film by the unforgettable Audrey Hepburn. And most importantly, he was on the verge of making literary history with his novelistic non-fiction work *In Cold Blood*, based on six years of close research into the murder of a Kansas family.

But *Answered Prayers* was never delivered, though Random House kept extending the deadline (and raising the promised advances). Nor did Capote ever admit that the book was not being written. On the contrary, he gave the impression, in his interviews and elsewhere, that it could reach the publishers any day, relating chapters and dialogues to editors and friends. When the chorus of criticism for non-delivery of the book got to him in the mid-1970s, Capote brought out four chapters and published them one by one in *Esquire* magazine.

As it turned out, this was not a wise decision. The rich and famous set in which Capote moved was scandalized by the revelations in the chapter entitled 'La Cote Basque'; Capote had told their lives, warts and all, sometimes not even bothering to disguise names. Jackie Kennedy was 'an artful female impersonator impersonating Mrs Kennedy'; the Kennedy men were 'like dogs—they have to pee on every fire hydrant'; Faulkner was 'Lolita-minded'; Sartre was 'wall-eyed, pipe-sucking, pasty-hued' and so on. Capote did not spare his 'swans'—the beautiful, intelligent, stylish set of women whom he liked to escort, and whose confidence he won. Not surprisingly, he lost his set of friends post-haste but was unrepentant. 'What did they expect,' he said. 'I'm a writer and I use everything. Did all those people think I was there just to entertain them?'

Capote did not blame the public outcry for his inability to finish the book; rather, he blamed his loss of form, a crisis of creativity. It altered the way he looked at art and life. He worried about the difference between 'what is true and what is really true.' He obsessed over how a writer could apply within a single form all that he had learnt from every other form of writing. He read all that he had ever written and was convinced that he had not fully exploited the aesthetic value of the material that had been in his possession. He laboured to relearn his art so that he could use at will, or even simultaneously, all he knew about the art of writing of poetry, reportage, plays, short stories, novels.

In any case, when he died in 1984, *Answered Prayers* was not complete and several theories exist about the truth of the matter. One belief is that the missing chapters are in a safe deposit box. The second is that they were never written. But the most credible view—since he used to quote widely and consistently from the missing chapters— is that they were written and, at some stage, destroyed.

Even in its curtailed form, *Answered Prayers* opens up a richly layered literary world. Capote's progression from being 'a spiritual orphan, like a turtle on its back', to a job in *The New Yorker* 'sorting cartoons and clipping newspapers' to celebrity status, with his face on so many magazine covers, is the stuff of legends on a scale that only American literary lions—Fitzgerald, Hemingway, Mailer, Salinger, Vidal—could achieve. Add drink, drugs, homosexuality and self-professed genius and the mix becomes almost too powerful, right up there with Marlon Brando, Sylvia Plath, Jack Kerouac. (Incidentally, it was Capote who made that withering comment about Kerouac's masterpiece *On the Road*: 'This is not writing, it's typing.')

But when the romance fades, when all the drinking and hangovers are done and all the bright lights switched off, one must look for the true test of genius, the actual work. And Truman Capote left behind a remarkable body of literature. When he died at fifty-nine, the *New York Times* described him as a writer 'whose prose shimmered with clarity and quality'. Capote combined brilliant reporting with lyrical writing, sensitivity with linguistic originality, to achieve his objective of writing simply, 'clear as a country creek'. William Shaun, editor of *The New Yorker*, paid him a huge tribute when he said, '... what seemed to mean most to him of anything in the world was words and sentences.' Such a man could not have had much wrong in him.

Recounting his ambitions in 1978, Capote said that he always knew he had to be successful, and he had to be successful early. He also knew that he wanted to be a writer, and rich and famous. Having achieved it all, and paid for it in many ways, he probably also understood well the meaning of St Teresa's statement: 'More tears are shed over answered prayers than unanswered ones.' Hence the title of his unfinished book.

Poet of the Hopeless

I remember well that December evening in Moscow when I picked up a fresh copy of the slim volume of Chekhov's short stories that I have re-read over the last month. The snow was falling thick and fast in the yellow street light as I emerged from the shop and soon it lay fresh and soft on the street and the sidewalks and on the sloping roofs of grim buildings. Much had changed in the city, I was told. The lights were bright, the shops were full, there was a new way of life. But in that luminous twilight it all seemed strangely familiar, as if three decades had not passed since the time I used to walk the city day after winter day.

The winter was thick with the same conspiratorial romance. The crunch of the fresh snow underfoot, the hurrying heavily clad figures, the snatch of music from some open doorway, lovers holding hands on cold stone benches, the drunken lurch from some bar with a chain across the door, the eternal prophetic hands of the Kremlin clock, all seemed familiar and friendly. Youth, it seemed, was still at hand; life was still a promise.

And as the snow fell, fragments of a long-forgotten poem, written under the sway of some youthful vision, began to float back into memory:

When
the river froze
Under its massive bridges
And water formed ice
For cars to slip.
Men
of pensive granite
Wore hoods of white
And planes sought lights
In snowbound nights.

The streets were still the same; their names had changed. The one I stepped onto, clutching my precious Chekhov volume, used to be called Gorky Street. Monuments to two great poets punctuated it at polite distances—one to the iconic Pushkin, whom one nineteenth century Russian critic called 'our everything', the other to flaming Mayakovsky. Through the doors nudged open by memory, Azerbaijani music floated down a sweeping staircase and pulled me in. The drums began to beat, a deep-throated song of the steppes broke out, there was the careless shuffling of young feet on the wooden dance floor, the flash of a forever smile from a raven-eyed beauty. Eternal friendships were being sworn over flasks of vodka, semi-sweet sparkling wine celebrated so many things that were beyond recall at dawn.

At one end of the same street was a tall building now reduced to dust and yet I saw it rise before me in the falling snow. On its twentieth floor was a small bar, with four little tables and stools. It had lace curtains on the windows and on the counter there was a pyramid of open sandwiches of black bread, red and black caviar, and peppered salami, prepared by a barmaid not unwilling to sit down at the round tables, take a cigarette, sip a drink and laugh.

On many afternoons here, I made friends of casual strangers and penned vagrant poems on paper napkins, comforted by the constant gurgling from the coffee machine.

Some time in that winter of more than three decades ago, on some afternoon when it became too tedious to trudge through the snow, I entered the world of Chekhov. Story after story, written with the directness of a medical doctor and the wistfulness of a poet, reflected what I saw around me—the everydayness of Russian life, the vanities and hopes of non-heroes, the fickleness, the fecklessness of human nature. I began to meet his characters everywhere: the doorman who took me to his one-room apartment and told me that he was actually a professor of mathematics and could speak Chinese but preferred to just clean the snow and spend the rest of the day as he liked; the middle-aged

Russian woman who caught me by the elbow in Tretyakov gallery one afternoon and would not let go until she had explained each painting to me, complete with quotes from Pushkin and Lermontov; the army officer who wore his uniform and decorations and drove his car around like a private taxi.

Everywhere, against the immense beauty of the Russian landscape, where the winter sun always hung low, they were living out the little ironical dramas of their lives. In celebrating the ordinariness, in raising the portrayal of the unremarkable to the level of world literature, Chekhov was echoing Gogol, who had said that for a successful short story, all a writer needs to describe is his own apartment.

At an amazing pace, Chekhov rolled out 600 stories, many of them very short, some hardly more than sketches. These stories drew their emotional impulse not from a plot but from character. The struggle, the crisis, the resolution were often not there, or internal. In that, Chekhov was a bridge between the structured realism of Maupassant and the psychological modernism of Joyce.

Hemingway once said that Chekhov wrote only six good short stories. But an entire generation of short-story masters inspired by Chekhov differed with that judgement. In Chekhov's stories, Gorky felt, 'everything is strange, lonely, motionless, helpless. The horizon, blue and empty, melts into the pale sky, and its breath is terribly cold upon the earth, which is covered with frozen mud.' For Nabokov, Chekhov wrote, 'the way one person relates to another the most important things in his life, slowly and yet without a break, in a slightly subdued voice'. And many others—Virginia Woolf, William Faulkner, John Gardner— acknowledged the Russian master who had made mood the predominant vehicle of conveying emotion, who said everything by leaving out more than he put in. And so, in that faraway winter, as over the last month, the slim volume proved the truth of V.S. Pritchett's words that the real short story is 'something glimpsed from the corner of the eye, in passing'.

Storyteller of the Sea

From my room in The Oriental hotel, I can gaze endlessly at the muddy Chao Praya, as it flows sluggishly past the concrete and glass buildings as well as the golden ornate pagodas of Bangkok. By day, the small powerful tugboats pull an endless procession of loaded barges to their industrial destinations and at night, when the dinner cruise boats begin to float, the river becomes a party. It is a strange river: it changes direction often, sometimes twice a day, depending upon the tides in the Gulf of Thailand. It was on this river, then known as the Menam, that the *Melita* came up in January 1888, carrying on board one of English literature's greatest prose stylists, Joseph Conrad, excitedly looking forward to his first command at sea.

The thirty-one-year-old Conrad had already seen a lot. Born nearly 160 years ago in 1857, under a Sagittarian sky, Josef Teodor Konrad Korzeniowski had followed his Polish parents into political exile in Russia when a child. He was an orphan by age eleven and a seaman on a boat from Marseilles at sixteen. Soon he was involved in gun-running for the supporters of a Spanish pretender—the experience was to be later fictionalized in *The Arrow of Gold*—and then obsessed by self-doubt, he attempted to kill himself. Fortunately for English literature, the bullet passed clean through his chest and he survived to sail as second mate and then first mate on British merchant ships to the Far East. In 1886, he received two certificates, one that made him a British citizen and the other that made him competent to be Master of a ship. And along the way, the man who was to go on to write *Heart of Darkness*—a journey not only into the heart of the African continent but into the depths of the human soul—also acquired fluency in the English language at the age of twenty-one. He would speak the language all his life with a thick Polish accent, but he would write it like a master, all the more amazing since it was his third language. His influence can be found in later modern masters—Hemingway, Greene, D.H. Lawrence, Powell ... and many would acknowledge his contribution to English prose. T.E. Lawrence wrote: 'He's absolutely the most haunting thing in prose that ever was: I wish I knew how every paragraph he writes goes on sounding in waves, like the note of a tenor bell, after it stops.' Conrad's own ambition was far more direct: 'By the power of the written word to make you hear, to make you feel ... before all, to make you see. That, and no more, and it is everything.'

But when he reached Bangkok, the iron barque *Otago* was not quite ready. For two months Conrad waited, supervising the loading of the ship and waiting for the malaria-ridden sailors to recover their health. He spent many evenings at the bar of The Oriental, trading tales of the sea, much like

Marlow, his fictional alter ego and narrator of many of his tales. He wrote: 'We talked of short rations and of heroism ... and now and then silent altogether, we gazed at the sights of the river.' And what he looked upon can be found in his fine late novella, *The Shadow-Line*: 'There it was, spread largely on both banks, the Oriental capital, which had as yet suffered no white conqueror; an expanse of brown houses of bamboo, of mats, of leaves, of a vegetable-matter style of architecture, sprung out of the brown soil on the banks of the muddy river.'

When the *Otago* finally weighed anchor and set sail for Singapore, difficult days were to start for the young captain and much of that experience has gone into *The Shadow-Line*, the line that marked the 'change from youth, carefree and fervent, to the more self-conscious and more poignant period of maturer life.' The experiences of that voyage and the underlying moral issues—the realization of one's weakness, the limitations of one's actions against human destiny, personal culpability, human courage under test— floated around in Conrad's mind for a long time, needing to 'be caught and tortured into some kind of shape.' First conceived under the title 'First Command,' the novella was finally written under its more philosophical title as late as 1915. Conrad spent less than a year in the region but so deep was the impact of this set of experiences that the material appeared in varying forms in many books—*Lord Jim, The Secret Sharer, Falk, The End of the Tether, A Smile of Fortune*—and over three decades. He himself recalled that the material of *The Shadow-Line* belonged to 'that part of the Eastern seas from which I have carried away into my writing life the greatest number of suggestions.'

He goes on to explain: '... it is personal experience seen in perspective with the eye of the mind and coloured by that affection one can't help feeling for such event of one's life as one has no reason to be ashamed of. And that affection is as intense ... as the shame, and almost the anguish with which one remembers some unfortunate occurrences, down to mere mistakes in speech, that have been perpetrated by one in the past.' As good an answer as any to that perennial question that every author faces: 'Is it autobiographical?'

Today, The Oriental has an Author's Lounge, with white walls, leafy plants and colonial wicker furniture. Here one can have a peaceful old-fashioned cup of tea with delicately baked cakes and listen to mention of other writers who have stayed here—Noel Coward, Somerset Maugham, Graham Greene ... But one look beyond the window towards the muddy river, already dissolving in the twilight, and there is no doubt. There could be Lord Jim on that wharf, Marlow could be lighting up a pensive cigar on that silent verandah, about to begin a tale among the buzzing of the thousand evening insects: the place belongs only to Konrad Korzeniowski.

Not Such an Idle Fellow

To the writer of a column called 'Second Thoughts', it should have long occurred to read a book called *Second Thoughts of an Idle Fellow*. Especially if the book has been lying obligingly on his bookshelf, simply asking to be picked up. Perhaps it escaped notice because of its modest appearance—unassuming, self-effacing, whispering like wealth but not talking like money. Content in its blue cardboard binding with grey cloth spine, reminiscent of my high-school calculus textbook and so unlike its other nineteenth century companions on the same shelf, all dressed up in their vintage finery of maroon leather and golden lettering. But once one gets beyond the covers, the charm is overpowering. Fraying edges of old thick pages, fragile to the touch, a large comfortable font and water stains that seem to indicate that it was rescued from some flood and left to bake in the sun for many days. And bought by—or more likely, gifted to—one Annie E. Albright, she of the slightly back-slanting handwriting, on Christmas 1898.

Chapter after chapter is vintage Jerome K. Jerome (the K stands for Klapka, a tribute to family friend and hero of the 1849 Hungarian war of independence, General George

Klapka). Reams of chuckle-inducing humour, laced with acid observation of human behaviour. He muses 'On the Art of Making up One's Mind', bringing home with pointed veracity the difficulty that a lady may have while choosing between a red or a grey hat or a gentleman standing in front of his wardrobe, wondering whether a tweed suit or a formal black one or a riding costume would present him as more imposing and admirable. He goes on to dwell 'On the Disadvantage of Not Getting What One Wants'. We learn about the 'Delights and Benefits of Slavery' and there are a full twenty-five pages 'On the Care and Management of Women'. In this last, he advises young men against a quiet, long honeymoon where the wife has enough time to examine, criticize and reform. Instead, the preferred option should be a whirlwind honeymoon during which the couple rushes across many cities, with many trains to catch and much luggage to pack. 'Don't give her time to criticize you until she has got used to you. No man will bear unprotected exposure to a young girl's eyes. The honeymoon is the matrimonial microscope. Wobble it. Confuse it with many objects. Cloud it with other interests. Don't sit still to be examined.' As part of his thoughts 'On the Time Wasted in Looking before One Leaps', Jerome describes the difference between a man and a woman leaving the house—the man simply shouts a goodbye, slams the door and is on his way, while a woman plans for it at least a day before, washes her hair, decides not to go, and then to go, kisses all the children …

A rollicking description of a pony pulling a cart after it has been given a pint of old ale on the advice of a meddlesome stranger makes a telling point 'On the Inadvisability of Following Advice'. And so on. The gems tumble out of this old book, coated in humour, stuffed with wisdom.

Jerome K. Jerome himself said: 'It is as the author of *Three Men in a Boat* that the public persists in remembering me.' He had no reason to regret on that account; on that score alone, his reputation in modern literature is secure. *Three Men in a Boat* (to say nothing of the dog) is a masterpiece of humour, quite simply the funniest book that one can ever hope to come across in the English language and one that should never be allowed to go beyond arm's reach. A page or two is guaranteed medicine against the severest bout of blues and a quick dip into it is the surest way I know of turning heartbreaking sobs into helpless chuckles.

Yet, Jerome must be permitted a momentary twinge that the public knows next to nothing of much else he wrote— several novels, collections of short stories, humorous essays, stage plays. Most have faded into obscurity or been dimmed by the fame of *Three Men in a Boat*, yet some ring a bell. *Three Men on the Bummel* (its American edition is simply *Three Men on Wheels*) that captures in hilarious detail a cycling trip in Germany, *The Diary of a Pilgrimage*, and the predecessor to the present *Second Thoughts*, *Idle Thoughts of an Idle Fellow* (1886), can still be found in bookshops. The fourteen essays in *Idle Thoughts* ... were all written as contributions to a regular column in a journal called *Home*

Chimes and proved to be so popular that they came out as a hardbound collection which sold, in Jerome's words, 'like hot cakes'. An informal, chatty, conversational voice that could weave effortless prose around subjects such as vanity, love (love is like the measles, we all have to go through it), weather, cats and dogs, babies and so on, had broken through the stodginess of Victorian prose. Jerome had few pretensions, not even to being a humorist, and often gave in to the temptation to sentimentalize and philosophize. Yet the vein of humour that he mined was so rich that it refused to be hidden away. 'What readers ask now-a-days in a book,' he wrote in his preface to *Idle Thoughts of an Idle Fellow*, 'is that it should improve, instruct and elevate. This book wouldn't elevate a cow. I cannot conscientiously recommend it for any useful purpose whatever.'

Besides producing an impressive body of fiction, plays and essays, Jerome edited two journals for several years *The Idler* and *Today*, and lectured extensively across Europe. Pretensions aside, idleness to him clearly did not mean lack of work. Yet the desire to wish away work, the claim to being joyfully idle, surfaces several times in his writings. At one place he says: 'I like work; it fascinates me. I can sit and look at it for hours. I love to keep it by me; the idea of getting rid of it nearly breaks my heart! It is the evasion of work that gives idleness its delicious quality: 'there is no fun in doing nothing when you have nothing to do.'

In the Land of the Panjachinar

For a panic-stricken moment, just before a short trip to Kabul, no book on Afghanistan comes to mind. Then suddenly, as the news spreads across the bookshelves, they stumble out, like old men being invited to visit a childhood haunt. From the back rows and from under forgotten piles, they emerge: Eric Newby, Robert Byron, Peter Levi, an old issue of *National Geographic*, and Babur himself. Eager companions on a flight over a hard-bitten landscape—brown plains, deep gorges, precipitous ranges covered with winter snows magically arranged by whimsical winds, narrow valleys with their hint of a river and that sign of human fortitude, a terraced field.

The cold in Kabul is clean and crisp. It gets quickly to the bone. The leafless skeletons of poplars and panjachinars stretch thin arms towards the sky, blue for only a brief while and then white, indistinguishable almost from the snow on the hill beyond. The eye searches for a patch of colour, but it is rare.

A man in a blue overcoat and a grey fez, an odd picture of old-world elegance against the gritty background of sentries, check-posts and guard dogs, rushes home. A

young girl waits on a deserted windy street, her black shawl bunched to her flushed face with her hands.

All too soon the sun decides to pack up for the day. The mountains pull their white covers over themselves; the only sign of their existence are the occasional brown ghostly ridges, calligraphic forms written by a heavenly hand. The snow begins to fall and it falls all night. In the morning the large flakes have settled softly into the cradles of pine needles on the tree outside the window. Dried mulberry and soft walnuts are served beside blazing log fires. And as the warmth spreads, it's easy to understand the lure that this land has long held for explorers and travel writers.

A few were allowed to travel inside the country after the First World War. Among them was *National Geographic*'s Maynard Owen Williams, the man who had once visited the tomb of Tutankhamen. Restricted to a six-mile radius around Kabul, he was given special permission to visit Bamian and, engrossed in his photography, nearly fell off the brow of one of the now shattered Buddhas. Williams has left behind, in a 1946 article, memorable snapshots of Kabul in 1941, where even the prime minister rode a horse and camels outpaced gaily decorated lorries. He recalls women in white burqas with modestly revealed two-tone sandals, turbaned fruit-sellers with amiable eyes, surrounded by bright red apples, yellow melons and festoons of lady-finger grapes, birds in quilted cages in soft-carpeted shops and bare-limbed poplars. Walking on the black ice on Chicken Street today, it seems half a century has not changed too many things.

Robert Byron, in his 1930s classic *The Road to Oxiana*, does not pause too long in Kabul, reserving his best prose for the charms of Herat. He and his companions are delighted to find a hotel that has writing paper in each bedroom but disappointed with a German shop that refuses to sell them hock without a permit from the minister of trade. The British legation, which today lies in disuse, was then furnished like 'home ... without any mosquito nets or fans to remind us of the Orient'. The Englishness was completed by roses in full bloom—with the local ministers vying for cuttings—a garden full of sweet williams, canterbury bells, columbines and tennis with six uniformed ball boys. Only a purple mountain beyond reminded the travellers where they actually were. Perhaps it is the pollution today, but I could not discern the sweet smell of the small yellow-green oleaster flowers that so decisively defined Afghanistan for Byron.

The same garden also captivated Peter Levi, travelling forty years later to Kabul in the company of Bruce Chatwin.

For Levi, Kabul was 'an untidy town surrounded by wheat fields like rough mats and by grey and black mountains still fretted with snow at the end of June'. His writing may lack the grace and light touch of Chatwin but makes up with sheer hard work, exploring and describing each region of Afghanistan. Levi's account, 'The Light Garden of the Angel King', draws its title, a trifle inaccurately, from the inscription above the Shahjahani mosque, made from grey Kandahar marble, just below Babur's grave. One can imagine Levi musing, his well-thumbed copy of the *Baburnama* in hand, 'with awe and almost with disbelief' among the mulberries and the ancient panjachinars, their trunks gouged with Persian graffiti.

'Within a day's ride from Kabul', writes Babur, 'it is possible to reach a place where snow never falls. But within two hours one can go where the snows never melt.' On the day we visit Bagh-e-Babur, there is snow everywhere. The terraced gardens, the surrounding walls, the caravanserai, the water channels, are all being given a new lease of life. 'Kabul's rhubarb is excellent. The quinces and plums are also good, as are the citrus fruits. One variety of grape, calledab-angur, is superb. Kabul wine is intoxicating', said Babur. Five centuries later, his beloved fruit trees are being planted again in the garden. The swimming pool, described by Williams in 1946 as 'gold flecked by autumn leaves' beside which he saw wives of foreign diplomats sunning their brown backs, is no longer there. All this would surely have pleased the king who conquered Delhi but wanted to be buried on this hillside in Kabul, under an open sky. To quote Mulla Muhammad Talib Mu'amma'i, whom Babur himself quotes:

> Drink wine in Kabul citadel, send round the cup again and again
> For there is both mountain and water, both city and countryside.

Song of the Road

Call it a leftover fantasy of youth, or perhaps the last burst of middle-aged angst, but I still want to do a Kerouac. Just pick up the old tan leather bag that I bought on Janpath a quarter of a century ago, throw in a couple of plaid shirts and a pair of jeans, pull on woollen socks and the walking shoes that have served so well for two decades, pick up all the spiral notebooks that are gathering dust and step out into the night.

Walk in whichever direction the stars order, stick out my thumb at passing lorries, drive along unknown highways past wheat fields luminous under a moody moon, talk all night with complete strangers, watch the wondrous miracle that is every dawn and meet life as it comes. Then survive to write about it, turning mounds of scribbled notes, snippets of conversations, random descriptions, into book after book of poetic prose, the outpourings of some footloose prophet of the road. It may never happen, I know. But such dreams are dear and must be kept, carefully folded away, never quite forgotten.

Like my copy of *On the Road*, an old one-franc copy held together with tape, bought one long-ago autumn morning, from the bin outside Shakespeare and Company, the bookshop to beat all bookshops on the left bank of the Seine. I read it again these last three nights, in a rush, much like it has been written.

Literary legend that has coalesced around Kerouac has it that the first version of the book was written on a high of benzedrine and coffee in three weeks on a single roll of unbroken paper. Kerouac had not paused to plan or fictionalize or edit. He had decided to write about his mad journeys across the American vastness, following the blue haze that only inveterate travellers know, just as they had happened.

And about his friends, those who were to become the other iconic figures of the beat generation—the crazy, frenetic, street cowboy—'a western kinsman of the sun'—called Neal Cassady, the poets Allen Ginsburg and Gary Snyder, the novelist William S. Burroughs. Kerouac went after them because they were his kind of people, 'because the only people for me are the mad ones, the ones who are mad to live, mad to talk, mad to be saved, desirous of everything at the same time, the ones who never yawn or say a commonplace thing, but burn, burn, burn like fabulous yellow roman candles exploding like spiders across the stars ...'

With Cassady, Kerouac criss-crossed America several times—hitch-hiking, driving, riding freight trains—convinced that 'somewhere along the line ... there'd be girls, visions, everything; somewhere along the line the pearl would be handed to me'. There certainly was everything, as *On the Road* describes in plainly spoken detail page after page—many girls, many drunken nights, stolen cars, fights, poetry, beautiful epiphanies, sadness, lonely moments, night after night of crossing endless deserts, happy fields, lost one-horse towns, ghostly wide rivers, all under stars 'as lonely as the Prince of the Dharma who's lost his ancestral grove and journeys across the spaces between points in the handle of the Big Dipper trying to find it again'.

Strongly influenced by Thomas Wolfe (*Look Homeward, Angel*), jazz and his dabbling in Buddhism, Kerouac had written an early formal novel *The Town and the City*, which met with modest success. But it was with *On the Road* that his influences came into full play and he discovered his talent for spontaneous prose. This was the 'sound of the mind' in which the first thought is the best thought.

It was not that his style found a ready market. For seven years *On the Road* remained only a manuscript in a rucksack. It was only when the other Beats—Ginsberg and Snyder—who had already achieved some literary fame, kept pointing to Kerouac as the best writer amongst them that the publishers took notice. The book instantly became a huge literary success.

Kerouac was the undoubted king of the Beat generation—the epithet for the group had been given by Kerouac himself. Beat originally meant weary—little wonder, given the pace at which they lived life—but soon became a concept much like hip, cool, square. Teenage adherents were called beatniks—remember, those were the days of the Sputnik.

Kerouac found it difficult to handle celebrity status. He seemed to need to live up to the images of *On the Road* and began to drink heavily—his favourite poison being jugfuls of rather sweet wine. He continued to write, following the same confessional style, even though his excesses had sapped his creativity.

Among the better works were *The Dharma Bums* (which made Zen Buddhism the accepted bohemian philosophy across America), *Big Sur* (written during a desperate retreat into nature), and *The Subterraneans* (written in three nights). But his spiritual and moral degeneration was a one-way street. In 1969, at the age of forty-seven, he died of abdominal haemorrhage caused by chronic alcoholism.

I may never live the Kerouac dream but there is some consolation in memories of a long time ago, of my first real journey away from home, scribbled in yellowing notebooks. Of travelling on the top bunk of trains across snowy vastness, of exhilarating conversations with strangers in old-fashioned dining cars, of eternal friendships promised over midnight wine in dark bars, of smiles that appeared like rainbows.

And when scarred and weary, but richer in the soul, I came back home, one of the books in my bag was this one-franc copy of *On the Road*, in which Kerouac had written: 'The bus roared on. I was going home in October. Everybody goes home in October.'

I looked at my ticket. It was dated 1 October 1983.

Memories in the Mist

Sometimes the very slimness of a book attracts. While there are times that one loves the feel of several tomes on the bedside table, each read to a stage marked by a bookmark cut carefully from some old greeting card, there are days when one wants the journey from cover to cover to be swift. It is in such a mood that I pick up what is not even quite a book. It is Monograph no. 18, put together in 1935 by Mr H.L.O. Garrett, the Keeper of the Records of the Government of the Punjab, bless him. Its title 'The Punjab a Hundred Years Ago' is fetching, particularly since Old Man Time, with his relentless assiduity, has piled on eighty more since Garrett made his effort.

The monograph contains the translated journals of two foreigners who travelled through Ranjit Singh's Punjab in the first half of the nineteenth century—Victor Jacquemont and Prince Alexis Soltykoff. Following in the footsteps of George Forster, the political agents Murray and Wade, Moorcroft, Emily Eden and several others, these two contributed a different sensibility.

Jacquemont was a young French aristocrat and naturalist on a mission from the Natural History Museum of Paris to explore the Himalayan region, one of his delectable tasks being a search for roses. He travelled from Calcutta to Delhi via Benaras and Agra, then to Simla and the Simla Hill States, right up to Tibet and then, finally, through Punjab and Kashmir. His journal, written in 1831, has ample evidence of his trained scientific mind and careful observation.

Soltykoff, a Russian artist from a distinguished family, came ten years later, sketchbook in hand, in search of exotic colour. He too covered Delhi, Simla and the surrounding hills and Punjab. The scientist met a keen and curious Maharaja Ranjit Singh at his zenith, who bombarded him with a hundred questions on politics, Bonaparte, science, medicine, God. The artist, known for his paintings of Sikh chieftains on elephants in motion, reached Lahore after the old Lion had passed on and the violent and bloody unravelling of his empire had begun. But of all that, some other time.

For the moment, this damp and misty morning finds me with the monograph on a relatively unspoilt hillside 20 km away from Simla. A massive cloud is flirting with the ridge on which stands Wildflower Hall, the one-time summer retreat of Lord Kitchener. The mist with the shadowy imprints of the deodars and pines creates a sense of timelessness and it is easy to imagine the Simla of the early days when Jacquemont came here. Having been set up only in 1815, the frontier outpost on the edge of Ranjit Singh's empire was quickly becoming popular with military and

civil officers of the Company, though it would be another thirty-five years before it would become the administrative summer capital of the Raj.

The Frenchman spent a year among the summer houses, drinking champagne and frolicking with dancing girls. 'Isn't it strange,' he said, 'to dine in silk stockings in such a place, to drink a bottle of Rhine wine and another of champagne every evening?'

He died, let us recall, of liver failure at the age of thirty-two, but not before he had managed to introduce the stately deodar to Europe. By the time Soltykoff came along in 1842 to 'this delightful mountainous spot, covered with forests, rhododendrons, pines (of which there are 16 or 17 varieties), firs and a kind of green oak', the station had expanded to house about 50 English gentlemen, 100 ladies and 'children in abundance' who passed the summers there to 'avoid more or less certain death in the plains'.

Though there was still no club or hotel, there was a general store 'where one can get anything' which serviced the several houses 'scattered among the trees, on the edges of precipices and on the peaks of mountains'.

Soltykoff took a large house for the season for 600 rupees, stocked it with beer and claret (not being able to stand the local favourite, brandy-pani) and hired twenty Indian servants, including a cook who, like any rest-house chowkidar, cooked 'plainly but well'. Regular milk supply was ensured by keeping six goats.

Soltykoff roamed the hills on one of his three horses or in a carrying chair called jampan, his 'almost naked' porters having been provided with uniforms. He spent six months painting portraits, reading *Don Juan* and visiting ladies whom he had come to know in Delhi or Agra and even attending a ball 'given on the occasion of the defeat of the Afghans, and the release of all the prisoners, the capture of Nankin, and peace with China'.

He seems to have been least perturbed by 100-strong groups of grey langurs regularly laying siege to his house in search of strawberries and raspberries in the garden and shows more emotion when expressing his distaste of mangoes, which reminded him of turpentine!

He had some harrowing adventures in the inner Himalayas and was glad to reach the plains from where he could admire the hills as a 'soft lilac outline seen against the rosy dawn.'

In the end, the artist much preferred the plains where he found 'grace and beauty for which one needs a hundred eyes and a hundred hands, to see all and paint all ...'

Wondering how long we would take to spoil this mountainside too, like we have the Simla of Jacquemont and Soltykoff, I put away the slim monograph.

The cloud has rolled down from the ridge, taking the entire hillside and valley in its embrace. It spreads its thin and wispy fingers through my open windows and comes in like a familiar neighbour. And the wind chimes begin their dance.

Reluctant Writers

The allure of a literary recluse is difficult to resist, particularly in a world where authors are falling over each other to be in the centre of the ever so transient spotlight and get themselves interviewed, photographed, awarded. The writer who can produce a masterpiece and then, instead of starting off on a multi-city book tour, just walks away from it all, sets himself apart from the pack and inevitably becomes a mysterious figure, the stuff of legends.

Quitting while ahead is easier said than done. And in recent times at least, nobody seems to have done it better than J.D. Salinger, the highly acclaimed and famously private author of the adolescent classic *The Catcher in the Rye* (1951). While the teenaged narrator of the *The Catcher ...*, Holden Caulfield, became one of the most successful characters of modern literature, the book met with controversy, critical acclaim and then ultimately commercial success, finding its way onto recommended reading lists of high schools and have-to-read lists of angst-ridden teenagers. By some count it still sells a quarter million copies every year; troubled adolescence is a forever theme.

There were other quick books from Salinger—essentially anthologies of his stories first published in *The New Yorker*—*Franny and Zoeey, Nine Stories, Raise High the Roofbeam, Carpenters and Seymour: An Introduction.* But he made a voluntary decision not to publish anything else after a story in *The New Yorker* in 1965. Legend, however, has it that he continued to write in his later years in a disciplined fashion, a few hours every morning, in his rural retreat in New Hampshire. The manuscripts reportedly piled up, with neatly labelled editing instructions, in floor-to-ceiling safes.

Nobody is to know the truth. Salinger was not interviewed since 1980 and he was rarely photographed or even seen. Moreover, he proactively resisted, at times through legal means, all attempts of biographers and publishers to bring out anything which would throw light on his personal life.

So intense was his obsession to keep away from the public eye that when *The Catcher in the Rye* was coming out in the US, he was hiding away in London. Nevertheless, he could not stop Joan Maynard's kiss-and-tell autobiography *At Home in the World* in which she talks about her love affair with the famous writer when he was fifty-three and she barely eighteen. This was followed by *Dream Catcher: A Memoir* by Margaret Salinger, the writer's daughter from his second wife. Margaret explores several Salinger myths including his interest in macrobiotics, homeopathy, acupuncture, meditation, Christian Science and so on. Actually, it's the song—*Here's to Life*—that best sums it up:

Hey there Salinger, what did you do?
Just when the world was looking at you
To write anything, that meant anything
You told us you were through ...

Other writers too have disappointed literary audiences after their first promise, either out of choice or otherwise. Ralph Ellison made a pioneering effort to explore black identity in 1952 with *Invisible Man* but could not complete his follow-up book. The intensely private Thomas Pynchon, who has never been interviewed, went silent for seventeen years after his early novels before becoming prolific again in the nineties. In fact, Pynchon's fans began to think that he did not exist, that he was actually Salinger, that he was only a computer programme!

But the reclusive shadow that I am chasing is Henry Green (actually Henry Yorke). Yorke was an aristocrat and an industrialist producing beer bottling machines. At night, in long hand, he wrote nine books that were to be ranked among the best in his time, rich with the legacy of D.H. Lawrence and Virginia Woolf. Fearing that he would be killed in the Second World War, he even wrote an early memoir, *Pack My Bag*, at age thirty-five. Though he survived the war, he could not handle the writer's block that set in thereafter and quit writing when he was forty-seven and well ahead in the game. He told an interviewer: 'I find it so exhausting now I simply can't do it anymore.' The man whom V.S. Pritchett described as 'the most gifted prose writer of his generation' took increasingly to drink.

He lost the directorship in his company to his young son, retired to his house, changed into his carpet slippers and just stayed in. He read novels borrowed from a department store, drank gin, let his teeth rot and watched sports programmes on television. He did not do any writing and allowed people to photograph him only from the rear.

But his slim body of work has made its mark. The novels—*Loving, Living, Blindness, Caught, Concluding, Party Going*—each title as clear as a pistol shot on a winter night, slip in and out of print. Critics and publishers may change their views about Green but fellow writers do not. If Somerset Maugham and the other Greene (Graham) are often called writer's writers, Henry Green is 'a writer's writer's writer'. No wonder he has been acclaimed as a genius by the likes of John Updike, Evelyn Waugh and W.H. Auden. I am halfway through *Loving* and it's easy to understand why. Clearly he demands more of the reader's attention than say, Greene.

Theme is a distant shadow, description is nominal and there is little by way of plot or overt action, though a lot still seems to go on. Gradually one discovers that the author has made himself invisible, letting the characters create themselves or fail in the process, refusing to sit on judgement upon them or setting up moral standards for them to meet.

Here one need not look for the story but for the rhythm of the prose, the quiet humour, unfailingly convincing dialogue, sensuous and fresh imagery.

His writing stands up easily to his own definition, a definition so true that I would like to pin it above my desk:

> Prose is not to be read aloud but to oneself at night, and it is not quick as poetry, but rather a gathering web of insinuation ... Prose should be a long intimacy between strangers ... It should slowly appeal to feelings unexpressed, it should in the end draw tears out of stone.

Silences of Shangri La

Sometimes things have a way of building up gently, unobtrusively. Serendipitous straws in the wind have been pulling me back to James Hilton, after a gap of three decades. First, there were the three nights in a Singapore hotel named Shangri La, where soft-footed attendants left not only the customary chocolate on my pillow but also a bookmark with a quotation from *Lost Horizon*. The quotation changed every night, and would do so, I was told, for the entire week.

Then, early on a crisp cold Sunday morning, I found myself on a plane descending into a bowl surrounded by sky-scraping snow-covered peaks, not too far, as the crow flies, from Hilton's setting for his 1933 novel, beyond the Kun Lun mountains. True, the town of Leh itself has no echoes of the peaceful, harmonious valley of Shangri La.

It is too full of tourists, cars, cell phones, several German bakeries, each proclaiming that it's the original one, sellers of beads and masks, travel agents and so on. But even there a visit to a lazy café brought forth a copy of *Lost Horizon*, left casually for the customer to leaf through and return.

But beyond Leh, there were enough moments that brought the evanescent and delicate dream of Shangri La to mind, like a once loved fragrance, long forgotten. Like that late evening when, in warm yellow light, we turned off the road above the Indus and walked into a hidden green crevice in the mountains. There, tucked away like a precious secret wrapped in silence, lay the monastery of Alchi, with its low structures, fruit trees whispering in the wind, a gentle lama or two, and a sense of the timeless. Or when a near full moon rose above the Stok Kangri peak, bathing in lambent luminescence the Indus valley with its ancient rocks and unexpected wild lavender patches and silver water and then, as if to make the magic incontrovertible, Venus and Saturn moved within kissing distance of each other. Or when a sylvan spot with green wild grass and shady trees and a gurgling brook appeared almost out of nowhere as if its entire purpose was to provide a haven to travellers who had driven for hours along the brown Shyok river, past the heat of the sand dunes of Hunder.

At these moments, and more, the name Shangri La nudged at the corners of the mind but one hesitated to use it, so hackneyed had it become and so used by hotels, restaurants, travel agencies, rock bands. The US

Presidential retreat in Maryland, the one called Camp David now, was called Shangri La by Roosevelt, and so was an aircraft carrier, and even a strip club in Florida! Several valleys have pseudo legends built around them due to their resemblance to Shangri La—the Hunza valley, places in Yunnan, Sichuan and Tibet, the Ojai valley where Frank Capra shot his 1937 film based on the novel. But as Hilton wrote: 'There is only one valley of the Blue Moon, and those who expect to find another are asking too much of nature.'

I cannot find my thirty-five-cent Cardinal Pocket Book edition of *Lost Horizon*, the one with the faint pink edging all along its pages, though I have the companion copy of *Random Harvest*, so old that it seems to have more sellotape than paper on its cover. Both were bought in 1977 from the piles of treasure that once used to mysteriously appear around Regal building. But there is a more recent edition, appropriately covered (does anybody still cover books?) in a blank patient's history sheet from a hospital in Bhutan—another destination too casually referred to as Shangri La. And from the very first phrase—'Cigars had burned low', Hilton weaves his spell, gently, until the reader, much like the hero Conway, steps into a dream, never sure whether the next step that he takes will fall on some ageless fantasy or on hard rock. The trance-like narration follows the story of Conway and his unlikely group of a missionary, a junior consular officer and an American swindler on the run into a remote and mysterious valley of incredible peace, harmony and beauty, ruled from a well-stocked lamasery, under the shadow of a conical mountain. But it would be wrong to read this book as an adventure novel: philosophical questions abound, revealed suddenly, discussed in calm contemplation while the moonlight caresses the ancient lamasery above the valley, lost in its mists. Conway discovers that the lamasery is devoted to collecting and protecting the delicate and beautiful things of life for a time when destructive passions will destroy the world, a time when the meek shall inherit the earth. Even youth and human beauty are protected because Shangri La has discovered the secret of incredible longevity.

Long after the slim novel has been put away, a haunting question remains: how much time is enough? What would an intelligent man do if, like Conway, he suddenly had the option to exist for centuries? There are the beckoning possibilities of a constant evolution of mind and spirit, the achievement of profundity and ripe wisdom and the enjoyment of 'long tranquilities during which you will observe a sunset as men in the outer world hear the striking of a clock, and with far less care'. How would it be if one had enough time, 'unruffled and unmeasured', to read without ever having to skim pages, listen to endless scores of music, indulge in the joy of 'wise and serene friendships, a long and kindly traffic of the mind from which death may not call you away with his customary hurry', or if solitude is what one prefers, then to endlessly enrich the gentleness

of lonely thoughts? But ultimately one can only agree with
Conway that for the mind to remain keen, the future must
have a point. 'I've sometimes doubted whether life itself
has any; and if not, long life must be even more pointless.'

Magic of the Green Baize

When authors and editors put their heads together to decide on the title for a book, it is not an idle moment. The title, perhaps more than anything else, will define the book, attract the eye or strike a resonance, at least at first encounter.

My bookshelf is sprinkled with books bought because their names touched a particular chord, brought back some shadowy time or promised a longer look at an evanescent haunting image. At least three of these books have been holding out a long overdue invitation to be read, an invitation that I seem to have resisted, ironically for the same reason that I bought them. Their names are so attractive and their appeal so romantic that any disappointment on their actually being read would be multiplied manifold.

Let me list out the names and let the readers judge for themselves: First, there is the hard-covered, royal blue-jacketed *None But the Lonely Heart* by Richard Llewellyn; second is the hard-covered, yellow-paged *Time and Time Again* by James Hilton and third is the slim Signet paperback, its pages edged in blood red, *Billiards at Half-Past Nine* by Heinrich Böll.

But this month, gathering courage, I picked up the last one. I recalled why I had bought it, in an unlikely second-hand shop in Berlin that had several neat shelves of books in English. It had brought back memories of a quarter of a century ago, when I had spent many evenings in a small district club, learning the mesmerising game of billiards from the dentist at the district hospital.

I watched, fascinated, as the good dentist, a chronic bachelor, smoothly stroked the white and red balls, forming true angles, impossible cannons, bold clean pots, kissing in-offs as the sun set over the western hills, leaving only a silver streak in the distance that could have been the Yamuna. When the low yellow light shone on the green baize, all the irrelevancies of life, the confusion, the question marks would fall aside and all truth, it seemed, could be translated in the way a particular ball was stroked. As I lost myself in Böll's path-breaking novel, that almost forgotten feeling was quickly reinforced.

The protagonist, Robert Faehmal, is closeted in the billiards room at the Prince Heinrich Hotel from 9.30 to 11.00 every morning except Sundays. Always alone, except for the bell-boy who listens to his stories, a glass of cognac and a carafe of water.

It is a sacred routine during which Faehmal tries to find some order in his existence in the predictability of the movement of the balls on the table, something that will make him forget the stupidity and meaninglessness of the war.

'Now gently, now hard he played the ball, seemingly at random, and each time, as it caromed off the other two, for him brought forth a new geometric pattern from the green void, making it a starry heaven. Cue ball kissing white ball over green felt, red ball over green felt, bringing tracks into being at once to be extinguished. Delicate clicks defined the rhythm of the figure formed, five times, six times, when the struck ball caromed off the cushion or the other balls. Only a few tones, light or dark, emerged from the monotone. And the swirl of lines was all angularly bound by geometric law and physics. Energy of the blow imparted to the ball by cue, plus a little friction, question of degree, the brain taking note of it, and behold, impulse was converted into momentary figures. No abiding forms, nothing lasting, all fleeting, force expended in a mere rolling of spheres.' The metaphysics of billiards can hardly be described better.

Billiards at Half Past Nine is an object lesson in the craft of writing. The tightly written 250-page novel is structured around one day, 6 September 1958. But through a brilliant control of the time perspective and fine characterization,

Böll packs into that day the experience of three generations of the Faehmal architects, along with their family and friends—in fact, the entire German experience from the Wilhelminian empire, through Weimar and Nazi Germany, to the West Germany of the 1950s.

The symbol that connects the three generations is the St. Anthony Abbey: the grandfather built it as a prize-winning twenty-nine-year-old architect at the beginning of the twentieth century, the father destroyed it as a reluctant twenty-nine-year-old demolition expert at the fag-end of the Second World War at the command of a Nazi General obsessed with clearing his 'field of fire' and the grandson is involved with its rebuilding. In an emblematic last scene, the grandfather's eightieth birthday cake arrives in the shape of the abbey and he cuts off its spire only to hand it to his son. In this simple act there is the compromise of generations, the reconciliation with a troubled but very real past, the rebuilding from the rubble, a colossal shrugging off of the question that haunts the novel—whywhywhy.

Böll's literary fireworks do not end there. The book begins when all that is worth telling in it has already happened. The stories are told in flashbacks and recollections. Lost times are brought back by following paths that go snaking into the undergrowth of the past with memory, which can be a curse or a blessing, as the only guiding light. Eleven of the characters delve into their memories, letting the events that they lived through, their recall of people and places, seep through their consciousness as deeply felt first-person narratives, often as fragmented, non-linear monologues.

The point of view changes with each chapter and with this rotation, every event is looked at from all sides and each character gets a chance to look at the others until gradually the layers form and the different dimensions develop into one seamless whole. The ultimate, brilliant effect is not unlike that of Robert Faehmal playing billiards 'with only one ball, white over the green surface, a solitary star in the sky. Light, faint music without melody, painting without likeness. Hardly any colour. Mere formula.'

Inspiring a Masterpiece

Normally I only glance furtively at obituaries; one never knows what, or rather, whom one may find in those columns. But the other day, glancing through *The International Independent*, I avidly read a half-pager on Dorian Leigh, the supermodel of the 1940s, captivating not only for her petite beauty, her Persian blue eyes and what *Vanity Fair* called her 'wayward lifestyle and reckless bravado' but more so for the fact that she was, according to literary legend, the inspiration for Holly Golightly, the winsome and eccentric heroine of Truman Capote's *Breakfast at Tiffany's*.

Whether she was the inspiration or not is probably a secret to all but Capote himself. When the novella was published he said that half the women he knew, and several whom he did not, claimed to be the inspiration for his main character, a phenomenon that he named the Holly Golightly Sweepstakes. Critics have even noticed a strong resemblance between Holly and Sally Bowles, the heroine of Christopher Isherwoods's story of the same name in his *Goodbye to Berlin* stories and the direct source for Liza Minelli in *Cabaret*.

Be that as it may be, Dorian Leigh, who became famous at around the same time as Vivien Leigh, certainly seems to have had much that would make up an inspiration. To begin with, she was clearly not just a pretty face. A bright school student and an English major, she went on to study mathematics at New York University and thereafter was busy doing mechanical drafting for the navy and designing aircraft wings when somebody directed her towards *Harper's Bazaar*. Her modelling career took off in no time and soon she was on the cover of *Bazaar*, to be followed by seven *Vogue* covers and another fifty on other major magazines. Her personal life seemed scripted to match: she married four times and among her many lovers were men of artistic distinction: the jazz musicians Dizzie Gillespie and Buddy Rich, the singer Harry Belafonte, the writer Irwin Shaw, the poet Robert Graves ... Inspiring enough?

Certainly I was inspired enough to go back to the book. In fact, so emblematic has been Audrey Hepburn's stamp on *Breakfast on Tiffany's* that one can be forgiven for wondering which was the original: Capote's 113-page novella or the 1961 movie. But the novella it is and the movie, however charming, must remain a derivative; in fact, in its making Capote felt double-crossed in every way since he had wanted Marilyn Monroe to play the lead. Mercifully, Paramount decided otherwise, else we would never have been left with that iconic picture of Hepburn with the cigarette holder.

Reading the novella in one sitting is like going back to one of those incredible days when, trousers rolled up to the knees, you walked into some crystal-clear and icy-cold mountain stream and reaching down picked up a handful of clean, chiselled pebbles and held them in your hand as the water slipped over them. So perfect is Capote's prose that each word feels like one of the pebbles and the narrative rushes seamlessly by. And almost unnoticed, New York enters through the open window: the eternal New York of dappled sunlight in Central Park, right-angled streets of brownstone apartment blocks, jazz notes floating out of summer windows, bars tucked away like surprises just around the corner, fancy shops on Fifth Avenue, chance romances, struggling writers, strange disappearances ...

None of this is surprising given that Capote was bothered not so much about what he wrote but the music that his words made, and he worked hard at it. Take for instance: 'Never love a wild thing. He was always lugging home wild things. A hawk with a hurt wing. One time it was a full-grown bobcat with a broken leg. But you can't give your heart to a wild thing: the more you do, the stronger they get. Until they are strong enough to run into the woods. Or fly into a tree. Then a taller tree. Then the sky. That's how you'll end up ... If you let yourself love a wild thing. You'll end up looking at the sky.' And then again: 'It's better to look at the sky than live there. Such an empty place; so vague. Just a country where the thunder goes and things disappear.' It is for writing like this that Truman Capote believed that his second career as a writer began with *Breakfast at Tiffany's*. Compared to his earlier, perhaps more evocative prose, he felt he had moved through 'a pruning and thinning-out to a more subdued, clearer prose ... more difficult to do.'

Capote would move on, constantly trying to reach a new perfection of writing, with his remarkable *In Cold Blood*. His unfinished *Answered Prayers* would lead him into controversy. But none of that would, or should be allowed to, touch the freshness, the verve and skill that are so evident in *Breakfast at Tiffany's*, inspiring Norman Mailer to call Capote 'the most perfect writer of my generation, he writes the best sentences word for word, rhythm upon rhythm. I would not have changed two words in *Breakfast at Tiffany's* ...'

And rightly so.

Wayward Wanderers

I step out without purpose, without destination. I step out merely because there is a sudden break in the seemingly incessant rain. The clouds have rolled back over the dark green mountains, like the curtains of some celestial stage, leaving only a wispy veil as a ghostly reminder of their presence. The late-afternoon sun has roared victoriously into the valley, turning every puddle, every tin roof into an incandescent fire.

The narrow path rises steeply under my feet, slippery with tufts of pine needles softened by the rain. Past a bubbling spring, harnessed by a villager's rough-and-ready drain pipe, and then it flattens out. The ranges, their silhouettes softened and rounded into an unreal gentleness, come into view. One curve follows another under the gaze of the deodars, their majesty broken every now and then by the impetuous sharpness of some maverick pine. It crosses my mind that I could walk on like this forever, one curve after another, a different view at each turn, a shifting of the light. I could drink from the garrulous springs; I could sleep under a sky overcrowded with stars. And perhaps it could all go into the notebook that I have always carried in my bag. And perhaps it could all form a book ...

As I retrace my bourgeois steps towards a warm dinner, I know where the thought comes from. From reading Laurie Lee and Knut Hamsun, not professional travel writers as one knows Paul Theroux or Eric Newby to be, but wanderer-poets—aimless, whimsical, charming.

Though he gained recognition as a poet, Laurie Lee is better remembered for his autobiographical trilogy, the second part of which is bewitchingly titled *As I Stepped Out One Midsummer Morning*. Here he describes how he left behind his Cotswold childhood (recalled earlier in *Cider with Rosie*), his mother's crowded cottage 'with rooks in the chimney, frogs in the cellar, mushrooms on the ceiling', and a deadening position as a junior in an accountant's firm. Bidding farewell to his mother on 'a bright Sunday morning in early June, the right time to be leaving home', he stepped out in search of 'mystery, promise, chance and fortune' on the road to London, carrying on his back 'a small rolled up tent, a violin in a blanket, a change of clothes, a tin of treacle biscuits and some cheese'. His hat gathered pennies as he played the street fiddler in towns and villages until he began to work in a builder's team in London. All along he fed his aspirations—writing poetry and hanging around Soho cafés, trying to look darkly international in his crumpled raincoat while he held the '*Heraldo de Madrid*, which I couldn't read, and order Turkish coffee, which I couldn't drink'.

Lee's wanderings took him to Spain simply because he knew how to ask for a glass of water in Spanish. This Galician journey, across a country of 'arid and mystical distances, where the sun rose up like a butcher each morning and left curtains of blood each night', is recorded in exquisitely lyrical prose, the prose that can be written only with a poet's eye. It began at the coastal town of Vigo, that 'rose from the sea like a rust-corroded wreck' and carried on through Valladolid, 'a dark square city, as hard as its syllables'. Drinking wine, playing music, scribbling poetry and conjuring romantic liaisons seemingly at will (Lee held an ineluctable sway over women all his life), he reached Madrid, the city 'with the lion's breath ... something fetid and spicy, mixed with straw and the decayed juices of meat'. As he walked on through Andalusia—with its magically named places—Cordova, Seville, Gibraltar, Castillo— he was already coming up against the beginnings of the Spanish civil war, brought home to the poet in him by 'just a whispering in the street and the sound of a woman weeping'. He was to come back later seeking an active role in the war, driven partly by his sense of adventure and partly by his passionate and doomed entanglement with a married woman—beautiful, demanding, jealous—who had become both his muse and his destroyer.

Knut Hamsun, the 1920 Norwegian Nobel laureate, was another one for wandering. Having spent his childhood a hundred miles north of the Arctic Circle—perhaps that had something to do with his spare, almost cold writing style—he tramped away his youth first in Norway and then as a street car attendant and farmhand in America, seeking literary success all the while. It finally came to him with the publication of his novel *Hunger*, an intense tale of a starving writer.

Hamsun was no armchair writer; he lived his philosophies. He worked on his farm, turning agrarian work into an act of individualism and seeing himself as an artist-farmer. His belief in the Nietzschean superman led ultimately to his open and unrepentant support for the Nazi regime, to the extent that he even handed over his Nobel medal to Goebbels. A huge financial fine and a censorship of his books followed the end of the War and literary revival has been understandably slow in coming,

though Isaac Bashevis Singer cites him as the founder of the modern school of twentieth century fiction, as Gogol was of nineteenth century Russian literature.

Politics aside, Hamsun's two closely interrelated novels, *Under the Autumn Sun* and *On Muted Strings*—brought together in a volume appropriately titled *The Wanderer*—make for intriguing reading. The middle-aged protagonist, perhaps 'a gentleman's son whom love had led astray' tries to escape from the city 'with its noise and bustle and newspapers and people' and seeks peace in rural solitude, humming to himself, 'caring for every stone and every straw'. The simple life that he seeks by drowning himself in whatever manual labour he can find on the farms continues to elude him, perhaps because his mind is not simple. And perhaps because of his tendency to fall in love with the wives or daughters of those who employ him. The protagonist's dramatic role model is a Mexican ranch hand who once talked in a deadpan voice, looking straight ahead, of a murder he had committed. Similarly, Hamsun's hero talks of complex romantic tangles—'and love is every bit as violent and dangerous as murder'—in a detached manner, even when he is deeply enmeshed in them. For the most part, he keeps his passions bottled up, preferring to wander away when fate does not smile. Emotion is conveyed surreptitiously—a silent vanishing, an inevitable return, a sidelong glance. My favourite line in the volume: 'A wanderer plays on muted strings when he reaches the age of two score and ten. That is when he plays on muted strings.'

Cairo from a Café

The night throws its canopy gently over the Great Pyramids at Giza, as if it were reluctant to smudge their sharp silhouettes. And as the first stars force their presence into a dusky sky, timelessness takes over the vision: there is an assurance that the pyramids are safe for another night as they have been for centuries. There is nothing more to be done there except to drive back into the heart of bustling Cairo and begin the search for the café where Naguib Mahfouz, the man who has been called Egypt's Balzac or Zola or Galsworthy, breakfasted and wrote for four decades.

It is not an easy journey. Even as the hour turns late, the streets are choked with cars, taxis and donkey carts piled high with large melons. We crawl past palaces and minarets, restaurants and shopping malls; clearly, there are no closing hours. And the night seems to be throwing a picnic for the entire city under the gently swaying date palms. On the bridge over the Nile, young couples, groups of young men, desperate fishermen, entire families in plastic chairs lean over as they gossip, watching the sparkling boats on their dinner cruises over the darkly rippling waters. And children, as always, clamber over the four huge lions that guard the bridge, once built for royalty.

Finally, we are at Tahrir Square, crowded and brightly lit, where everything seems to be happening at once. Café Ali Baba is right there, except that it is abandoned and boarded up. A traffic policeman gladly turns away from his impossible job and explains that the old café has been sold by its owner; a fast food establishment is soon to open in its place. Fast food in a place where men have sat for decades (and been joined by women only in recent years) to drink tea and coffee and pull at their water hubble-bubbles, exchange gossip, discuss revolutions and coups, play backgammon and dominoes and watch life go about its daily business in the square, the square about which Naguib Mahfouz once told an interviewer: 'The square has had many scenes. It used to be more quiet. Now it is disturbing but more progressive, better for ordinary people—and therefore better for me also, as one who likes his fellow humans.' I stare at the second-floor windows where Egypt's best-known literary observer would have sat in the early mornings: they are dark and shut, the end of many things.

My disappointment must have dripped from my face, for, my guide quickly said: 'There is another café, just like this one. Very old, and he used to go there sometimes too.' Literary pilgrims must be quick to believe such things, so I followed him deeper into the heart of the old city, past mosques and crowded squares, through narrow alleys, to the El Fishawy Café. Its rounded tables and chairs have taken over the alley occupied by the several grizzled old men who seem to have been sitting there forever, under the old carved mirrors, round fans and brass chandeliers, counting their beads and smoking their hookahs. The place clearly belongs to them, not to tourists who have their coffee, take photographs and continue their souvenir-hunting in the lanes beyond.

It is easy to imagine Mahfouz's 'Karnak Café', the café of the title of the angry novella set against the 1967 war. In that café, under the watchful gaze of the fascinating proprietress Qurunfula ('the roseate dream from the 1940s'), Mahfouz's troubled characters suffer in the difficult political circumstances of the times. It is a place, much like the one where I sip my mint tea, where 'you get to sense past and present in a warm embrace, the sweet past and glorious present.'

Virtually unknown beyond the Arab world until 1988, when the Nobel Prize brought instant international acclaim, Naguib Mahfouz had based his immense body of work on the three pillars of faith, love and politics—but politics 'is by all odds the most essential'. More than thirty novels, including the epic Cairo Trilogy, several short-story collections, screenplays and articles, all written in classical Arabic, created, as the Nobel citation notes, a work 'rich in nuance—now clear-sightedly realistic, now evocatively ambiguous ... an Arabian narrative art that applies to all mankind.'

Beginning at the age of seventeen, when he was surprised that an editor actually paid him a pound for a story ('One gets paid as well!'), and combining his writing with a day job as a civil servant, Mahfouz worked with a rigorous discipline to pack in as much reading and writing as possible: the early café mornings and the fact that he even put off marriage till the age of forty-three are evidence of that. In early novels he explored Egypt's Pharaonic past but his most memorable work chronicles, in fiction, Egypt's tryst with modernity in the mid-twentieth century. In novels such as *Cairo Modern*, *Midaq Alley* and finally the trilogy—*Palace Work*, *Palace of Desire* and *Sugar Street*—he examined the contradictions of a traditional society in the throes of change. The remnants of British influence, the degeneration of an authoritarian bureaucracy, rampant unemployment, student anger, militant nationalism, increasing radicalisation, all come under his steady gaze. Reading Mahfouz, one can understand the deprivation and the hunger that leads to revolutions in such a society, the disillusionment that follows (Mahfouz fell silent for five years after Nasser's 1952 takeover), the temptations of fundamentalism, the bitterness of defeat. As Edward Said wrote of Mahfouz: 'He has a decidedly catholic and, in a way, overbearing view of his country, and like an emperor surveying his realm, he feels capable of summing up, judging, and shaping its long history and complex position as one of the world's oldest, most fascinating and coveted prizes for conquerors like Alexander, Caesar, and Napoleon, as well as its own natives.'

As I muse over all this, the bazaar seems to have entered the El-Fishawy Café. Caps, shoes, beads, snapshut cigarette cases are all for sale at our table. A man almost forcibly takes my shoes to polish them. A waiter walks around with tongs and hot coals to replenish the hookahs. There is a call for a fresh ball of tobacco. It is well after midnight but life here does not stop by the clock.

Chronicling the Hills

There comes a point in every long-gestation literary project when one doesn't want to see it anymore. One hands it over to the editor with the fervent wish that he will do the rest and not send it back for more revision and rewriting, or for tinkering with voice and tone, or for taking out more favourite paragraphs. A blue folder left my desk two weeks ago with similar prayers, perhaps nine years after its first seeds had been sown. For a while at least I cannot be too worried about its future; a sense of relief overwhelms all other emotions. There is a perceptible lightening of the shoulders, an uncoiling of the mind. Suddenly, the horizon seems further away. The mornings seem to have an extra hour; the weekends are what they are meant to be. In such a mood it is difficult to even read anything that is demanding or intense. One searches for the languid prose that would speak of beautiful places, unhurried times. Four books on Dehra Dun and Mussoorie on my shelf present themselves.

Ruskin Bond's *Landour Days* with its dreamy blue watercolour vista of hills and valleys is first to hand. One can easily picture this understated chronicler of Mussoorie at work on this journal, sitting in his cottage on a typical

Landour morning: 'No water in the taps. No electricity until late afternoon. Telephone out of order. Postman comes by, but without any mail.' The absence of mail, and hence of cheques and acceptance letters, can have a poignancy of its own for a committed freelance writer. Bond's journal is a whimsical collection of stray observations, such as those on the mating habits of swifts and typical anecdotes that one can imagine being traded at the Writers Bar in the now-vanished Savoy Hotel, while long-robed ghosts of sahibs and memsahibs looked on.

Every once in a while there is the unmistakable flash of genius: 'The wind in the pines and deodars hums and moans, but in the chestnut it rustles and chatters and makes cheerful conversation.' Or in the description of the death of the peanut-seller who has sat at a Landour corner for decades, hunched over his little fire, 'as fixed a landmark as the clock tower or the old cherry tree that grows crookedly from the hillside. The tree was always being lopped; the clock often stopped. The peanut vendor seemed less perishable than the tree, more dependable than the clock.'

The peanut vendor gone, eternal questions left hanging in the air, Bond still walks Landour in the 'moonlight, starlight, lamplight, firelight ...' The night, as he says, is his friend; at night he can smell a leopard without seeing it, watch the prowling jackals or the flitting squirrels or the foxes dancing in the moonlight. Ruskin Bond may have forgotten it, but I remember well that summer morning forty years ago when I walked in unannounced, a young student, into his cottage and was presented a copy of his slim volume of poetry called *Lone Fox Dancing*.

The peanut vendor—he must be the same—makes an appearance again in Stephen Alter's affectionate recall of a Landour childhood, *All the Way to Heaven*, a book that touches one only as something written straight from the heart can. Alter sensitively evokes the life of the missionaries on the Landour hillside in the 1960s and 1970s, a time when hampers with fancy canned food and 'seconds' clothes still came from the West. A time when the shopkeepers came to take orders of the daily needs of custard and Ovaltine, of Dalda ghee and Brooke Bond tea, when the the razai wallahs, the Kashmiri wallah, the kabadi wallahs followed the egg wallah, the cheese wallah and the meat wallah all the way to the doorstep.

It's easy to relate to the young Alter feeling sick in his father's old Landmaster car, driving up the hairpin bends to Mussoorie and waiting to suck on the slice of lemon at the toll tax barrier. Or walk with him from Rajpur, past the ugly wounds of the limestone quarries, past the railway school at Jharipani, through the fresh bakery smell of Barlowganj and into the dark green deodar cover of Landour. Or lie awake at night listening to the orchestra of the cicadas building up only to be drowned by the hammering of the sudden monsoon rain on the corrugated roof.

It is easy, I say, because while Stephen Alter was growing up in Woodstock, I was doing the same in the schools of the valley below. So somewhere, through half-closed eyes, his memories begin to merge with mine. The black-and-white world of the 1960s, the lost forever world of childhood begins to come alive.

A world where we played Robin Hood and his Merry Men in a lush-green nullah outside the school. A world of watching Jerry Lewis comedies and John Wayne toughies and eating aloo tikki covered with imli chutney in the interval. Of weaving our cycles expertly through the crowded Paltan Bazaar until we reached the target of the black gulab jamuns made with atta, of risking our lives in the Chakrata Road traffic just to buy linseed oil and develop the 'stroke' of our cricket bats. Of buying new schoolbooks every year on Rajpur Road along with brown paper jackets, glue, pencils and those so expensive scented erasers. A world where one still had the time to make little paper boats and float them down the canals that rushed churning white down the hillside or to lie around in the sugarcane fields beyond the Rispana, chewing idly on juicy blades of grass ...

The canals have now become roads; the fields have changed into concrete residential colonies. The lazy, friendly town of tongas, litchi gardens and bungalows is changing into a crowded, rushing, concrete city. I don't even need to reach for the other two books still on my table. The world has caught up with Dehra Dun. But let me not lament its passing; let me instead celebrate its memories. As Ruskin Bond does when he writes: 'Dear old Dehra: I may stop loving you, but I won't stop loving the days that I loved you.'

Long Shadows of Short Stories

The sky is a splattered sunset orange. The sun, a blazing hoop of fire, balances itself on the taut line of the horizon and then sinks effortlessly into the sea. The swaying palm leaves make silhouettes and the last of the sailboats are heading, still aided by a strong breeze, homewards. The next time I look up, the orange of the sky has given way to many shades of pink and below it lies a tranquil sea, still heaving but in a tired, late-evening manner, without the vigour that had come roaring out of its heart in the morning and ended as churning white foam at the feet of grizzled old fishermen, waiting there with the dawn. I watch the colours change until everything, the sky and the sea, becomes only shades of blue and a thin crescent appears in the sky as if drawn by a sharp white pencil and the silhouettes turn sharper, darker. When I turn back it is already too late to read without a light.

But I have already read enough for the evening and there is that uncomfortable residual feeling that the mind is yet to absorb the nuances, the layers, the insinuations of all I have read. Three *New Yorker* short stories, more than what

I have dared to read in as many years. And clearly, it has been my loss.

'Gold boy, Emerald girl' by Yiyun Li is a story set in modern Beijing—too many cars, missing the old bicycles—a story of a middle-aged man raised only by a mother and a woman raised only by a father. It starts off innocently as an account of a date arranged by the man's mother between the two and ends as a story of three 'lonely and sad people' who could not make one another less sad but could make 'a world that would accommodate their loneliness', a screaming exploration of several themes: loneliness, old age, companionship, the dreams and fears of childhood, the absence of a parent ...

The second story, originally written in French by J.M.G. Le Clezio and called 'The Boy Who Had Never Seen the Sea', speaks to me in my surroundings. It begins with the dream of a young boy, obsessed with Sinbad, to find the wide blue expanse and proceeds to describe every mood, colour and smell that the mighty deep can have, and the human yearning to explore it, know it, befriend it, and the need to fear it, to survive it. The story ends with intriguing musings about the boy's future: 'Perhaps he really did go to America, or to China on a cargo ship that travelled slowly from port to port, from island to island. Dreams that begin like this never have to end.'

And the last story, entitled 'Sleep', is poetic and tender. It's about a man who loves to watch his wife sleep because she is beautiful and because he feels privileged that she can turn off all her defences in his presence. From the time that he moved in with her to the present when she is a grandmother, he has watched her sleep for twenty-five years, 'through the recession, the boom and now through the new recession'. And while he watches, and she sleeps, one can feel the ups and downs of an entire lifetime, the joys, the anxieties of marriage, of children, careers ... There is a time bomb tucked away; he has learnt that he has colon cancer, but he has not told her yet ... because the doctor told him that there was a good chance that he would not die, and because she is sleeping.

Just three short stories and so many worlds open up, so many questions to muse over. That is why these stories work, evidence again of the truth that what is said in a short story is perhaps less important than what has been left out, or only hinted at. The short story relies for its success on taut architecture, in which there is not a single idea or word which does not add to the tension of the narrative; unlike the novel, it has little place for the luxury of byways. One careless stroke, one aimless paragraph can spoil it all. Jorge Luis Borges, one of the masters of the form in the twentieth century, once wrote: 'Unlike the novel, a short story may be, for all purposes, essential.' But the essential has echoes and, in a good short story, these can be heard at quite a distance and most clearly when they resonate against something in our own lives. A good story need not always await momentous events or earth-shattering changes: the extraordinary strangeness of ordinary life is rich enough. As Chekhov perhaps best showed, each nondescript man can be a hero in his daily fight; moral ambiguity, doubt, passion and courage are not the preserve of only a few. All a short story needs at its core is a moment: enigmatic, immense, unique.

One of my eternal favourites, short and bittersweet, is Ernest Hemingway's 'A Very Short Story.' It's all of 633 words and I wish I could quote it in full. Hemingway tells the story, with autobiographical echoes, of an American soldier's love for the nurse who looks after him in an Italian wartime hospital, their desire to get married and the fifteen letters he gets from her when he is sent back to the front. When the armistice is signed, he goes back to America to get a job so that they can get married. She meanwhile meets an Italian major and writes to the American that theirs was 'only a boy and girl love' and it's best that they forget about it. But 'the major did not marry her in the spring, or any other time' and our hero contracts gonorrhoea from a sales girl. All the desperation of wartime love, the promise and the sweetness as well as the disappointment of youth, in two printed pages. But Hemingway could better himself. He wrote the shortest story in just six words to win, it is said, a $10 bet. The story, complete in itself, dripping with heartbreak: 'For sale: Baby shoes, never worn.'

Tips and Tales

In an entertaining and typically ironic talk in Delhi, Paul Theroux did at least two good things. First was the epiphany: Travel writers seldom go back to the places they have written about. Bruce Chatwin never went back to Patagonia. Graham Greene wrote the definitive travel book on Liberia after three weeks in that country (*Journey Without Maps*) and the definitive travel book on Mexico after a month there (*The Lawless Roads*) and never went back to either place. Theroux himself seems to suffer from no such inhibitions. A few years ago he retraced his epic journey recorded in *The Great Railway Bazaar* that had taken him in the 1960s from London's Victoria Station to Japan and back through the Soviet Union on the Trans-Siberian Express. The second time around he could not get a visa through Iran but had the compensation of discovering the several new Central Asian countries that had emerged in the meantime. So if he could not drive down the Khyber and take a train through Pakistan to Attari, he flew down to Amritsar from Tashkent—a city one should be able to see, according to Theroux, if only we bothered to stand on tiptoe and peep over the mountains.

And why do travel writers hesitate to return? Theroux rather let the question hang in the air, but when pushed agreed that one reason could be the fear of disillusionment, the possibility of being proved wrong. The essence of travel writing is the expression of a sense of place at a particular time and one may never be able to bring in all the elements of a moment together in the same way ever again. I wonder often if I were ever to visit Auschwitz again, would I feel the awesome silence and presence of monumental death that I had experienced late one summer afternoon, walking through the deserted camp-museum. Or the sense of ancient times that descended out of an incandescent blue sky amidst the sun-bleached ruins of Palmyra, while a small village boy, bribed with a pack of cigarettes, posed for photographs beside a camel. Or the romance of sipping black tea under the arches of an Isfahan bridge, where the waiters jumped over the flowing waters of Zayendeh rud, carrying ornate tea trays and refreshed hubble-bubbles.

The underlying point is undeniable. Much like one never steps into the same river twice, one can never quite visit the same place again. Something will inevitably be different—not only will the place have changed but so would the writer. In fact, it's much like visiting a childhood home—the cavernous rooms shrink, the mile-long driveway is not even fifty yards, the distant gate has moved so close.

Theroux's second good act of the evening was to sign for me two old books of his that I had carried to the talk. A perceptive bystander remarked that though the books were twenty years old, they were in excellent condition. I did not dare confess in the presence of the author that they were also unread. The reason: both the books—*The Consul's File* and *The London Embassy*—deal with diplomatic life. One likes to keep one's day job separate from the literary life, so having never written about life in embassies, I was a bit hesitant to read about it too. Theroux's generous autograph helped overcome that inhibition and yielded rich dividends.

Though Theroux, from all I know, has never spent time in an embassy, he reveals a deep inside knowledge of both the humdrum and the more glamorous side of a diplomat's life. In *The Consul's File*, he comes across as a sort of informal Somerset Maugham following a young American diplomat

who has been assigned to shut down a consulate in a remote outpost in tropical Malaysia. Ostensibly nothing much should happen in a place with a few shops, a dispensary, a school and a club with its unusable billiards table and leftover colonials. But the Consul finds the undergrowth is alive with tales of love, anger, deception, madness, ghostly visions, sexual scandal. And somewhat reluctantly he starts writing things down. 'I considered writing my last resort ... Of the three men in the Foreign Service I knew to be writers, two were failures in their diplomatic duties and the third ended up selling real estate in Maryland.'

The London Embassy is a follow up to *The Consul's File* and here Theroux's protagonist is seen facing the challenges of diplomatic life in metropolitan London, which can be quite different from those in a remote outpost. There are engaging and realistic vignettes of diplomatic life—a welcome reception where the home team sits down for a discussion after the guests have left (Now, how about a real drink?), the tension at the Ambassador's residence before the prime minister drops in for dinner, office politics generated by a telex operator who decides to wear one earring ... Mix these with adventures involving alluring property dealers and culturally minded ghouls and you have assured entertainment.

In contrast to his persona as a boundless traveller, Theroux does not emerge as a very ambitious fiction writer. The stress rather is on controlled craftsmanship. Stories are collected assiduously and told charmingly. They are linked together by a common character or neatly pinned between the frames of one diplomatic posting. Such craftsmanship is the dream of publishers. No wonder then that Paul Theroux has nearly fifty books to his name in less than those many years of writing!

Conversations in the Dark

To be quite honest, Isaiah Berlin, the Oxford political philosopher, has always seemed a bit too formidable to read. And except for one brave attempt three decades ago—which resulted in some vigorous underlining—I have let his book *Russian Thinkers* remain in mint condition on my shelf. But another of his books, recently to hand, seemed more inviting, complete with its yellowing pages, its old-book smell, black-and-white photographs and far friendlier title of *Personal Impressions*.

Charming is an inadequate word for the essays the book contains—elaborate, cultured, sympathetic and educated assessments of Churchill and Roosevelt, Chaim Weizmann and Albert Einstein, Aldous Huxley and Virginia Woolf. Berlin's own intellect, sensitivity and knowledge is the life blood of these essays but it is unobtrusive, almost unseen; there is no attempt to push the self into the picture. There is no 'lopping off the heads of the tall poppies', no deliberate attempt to look for weakness. Instead, there is an affectionate effort to decipher genius and in so doing, praise it; the driving force is redemption, not condemnation. As the introduction says: 'Like Hamlet he stands amazed at what a piece of work is a man; unlike Hamlet he delights in man.'

Berlin spent most of his life at Oxford, except for a brief stint at the British embassy in Washington in 1945. Being a native Russian speaker—he was born to a wealthy Jewish family in Riga and saw the 1917 revolutions in Petrograd—Berlin was asked to fill in a temporary situation at the embassy in Moscow. The friendships with Russian writers, particularly Boris Pasternak and Anna Akhmatova, which Berlin writes about in an enchanting fifty-page essay ('Meetings with Russian Writers in 1945 and 1956') began during that stay.

The context was dark: the country was war-ravaged, the years of the midnight knocks and gulags were not forgotten and would soon return, freedom of thought and expression was anti-revolutionary and contact with foreigners—particularly those from Western embassies—was fraught with mortal danger. But literary Russia was very much alive, available books were devoured, manuscript copies were circulated privately, poets were worshipped as heroes.

During the war, soldiers went to the front with the words of Alexander Blok, Mayakovsky and Marina Tsvetaeva on their lips, and both Pasternak and Akhmatova, who were living in internal exile, received piles of letters from the front quoting from their published and unpublished works.

Pasternak lived in his dacha at Peredelkino, a writers' colony not far from Moscow that had been organized by Gorky and it was there that Berlin met him on a 'warm, sunlit afternoon in early autumn'.

Many years later, I made the same journey but it was on a windy spring day, with the last remnants of snow welcoming the first green leaves and my destination was not the writer's house but his grave.

But to return to Berlin—he was the bringer of news from the world of Western literature and art to Pasternak and his friends, for whom time had stopped. Pasternak admired Proust and Joyce and asked if Malraux was still writing; he had not heard of Sartre or Camus and thought little of Hemingway.

But it was Pasternak's conversation that fascinated Berlin—'his talk often overflowed the banks of grammatical structure—lucid passages were succeeded by wild but always marvellously vivid and concrete images'. Like Virginia Woolf, Pasternak 'made one's mind race ... and obliterated one's normal vision of reality in the same exhilarating and, at times, terrifying way'. The essay also includes Pasternak's account of the famous telephone call from Stalin during which the dictator wanted to know if Pasternak was present when the poet Osip Mandelstam lampooned Stalin. Pasternak evaded the issue; Mandelstam died in Siberia.

In 1945, Pasternak had only completed a draft of a few early chapters of *Doctor Zhivago* but even then called it 'my last word, and most important word, to the world. It is, yes, it is, what I wish to be remembered by; I shall devote the rest of my life to it.' Berlin met him again after a gap of eleven years. By then the writer's estrangement with the political order was complete. His friend, Olga Ivinskaya, on whom *Zhivago*'s Lara is supposed to be modelled, had been sent to a labour camp for five years. During this meeting, Pasternak thrust a thick envelope containing the entire manuscript of *Zhivago* into Berlin's hands; it had already been smuggled out to an Italian publisher. The rest is literary history—the Nobel Prize in 1958 and his refusal under political pressure.

The account of Berlin's famous night-long meeting with Anna Akhmatova in Leningrad, a meeting which she believed set off the Cold War, must await another occasion, to be told at length unless, of course, readers can get their hands on *Personal Impressions* before that.

Tormented by a Restless Breeze

I do not believe that I am qualified to write on Faiz Ahmad Faiz. But the memory of a long-ago Moscow afternoon tempts me. As a young diplomat existing somewhere at the edge of the embassy, I could not believe the phone call from the multilingual and multi-talented Amina Ahuja, who happened to be the Ambassador's wife. 'Come with me,' she said, 'we will go and meet Faiz sahib.'

I could only ascribe the immense honour to an incident when, listening to some ghazals of Faiz at a colleague's house, she had noticed that I knew some lines by heart.

Soon I found myself being whisked away in unaccustomed elegance to the edge of the city, then through birch forests, to the immaculate green lawns of a hospital meant for those who mattered. A committed Marxist, Third World internationalist, poet of the oppressed and winner of the Lenin Peace Prize, Faiz was entitled to be there.

A walk down a long corridor and we were in the warm presence of the master, recuperating in his room with wife Alys at his bedside. I forget the exact conversation but, in a few minutes, Faiz had got up from the bed and we all walked out into the lawns, perhaps so that he could light his ever-present cigarette. And there he proceeded to recite some of his new poems ...

I did not fully realize then how weak and tired he was, ailing between his days in Beirut and his final return to Lahore. A boyish smile still lit up his deeply lined face, a denial of the sadness in his eyes. In a year and a half he would be dead. Today I rue the carelessness of youth that makes us think that life and people are forever ... else even in a non-digital age, there should have been a camera or, more important, a tape recorder.

The memory settles back into the comfortable crevice created by twenty-five years and I listen once again to an invaluable recording in his own voice—his deep, resonant, rhythmic, rasping smoker's voice—as he recited his poems for Dr Shaukat Haroon, believed to have been his muse for several of them, under the shade of a huge banyan tree at her residence in Karachi.

The famous

Gul-on mein rang bhare, baad-e-naubahar chale
chale bhi aao ki gulshan ka karobar chale

(Bring the flowers to bloom, let the spring breeze blow
Come, my love, and rouse the garden from its sleep)

sung to perfection by Mehdi Hassan, is believed to have
been written for Shaukat Haroon.

As, of course, the eulogy that he wrote when he locked
himself in a hotel room in the immediate grief of her death:

Chand nikley kisi janib teri zebai ka
rung badle kisi surat shab-e-tanhai ka

(Let the moon of your beauty rise from some quarter
and change the mood somehow of this lonely evening)

There were other loves and passions too as he revealed
in an unusual interview with Amrita Pritam, including
an unexpressed love at the age of eighteen. Faiz let that
experience flow into the poems in his first collection:
Naqsh-e-Faryadi, including the immensely evocative
verses in which the poet addresses his rival:

Tu ney dekhi hai vo peshani, vo rukhsar, vo hont
Zindagi jin ke tasawwur mein luta di ham ne
Tujh pe utthi hain vo khoi hui sahir ankhen
Tujh ko malum hai kyun umr ganwa di ham ne

(You who have known that cheek, those lips, that brow
Under whose spell I fleeted life away
You whom the dreamy magic of those eyes
Has touched, can tell where my years ran astray)

But his real love was Alys, an English girl who came to
India in the 1930s, already a member of the Communist

Party in London. In Faiz she found a soul mate. Theirs was to be a friendship and partnership of four decades, through thick and thin, through Faiz's imprisonment and self-exile. As Faiz told Amrita Pritam: 'Alys is not just my wife, but my friend as well. This has made life bearable for me. There is intense pain in love, but friendship is peace.'

Faiz's words in his own voice can cast a strange spell, can create a mood that reaches deep into the soul, leave behind visions and images, and a smouldering fire. That is why I have kept this recording at hand for years, much like Faiz himself never slept without *Diwan-e-Ghalib* by his bedside.

'No one can say he has read enough of Ghalib,' said Faiz. He adapted Ghalib's belief of expanding the particular to the general, to feel the sense of oneness with humanity expressed in Ghalib's couplet:

Qatray main dajla dikhain na day, aur jaz mein kul
Khel larkon ka huwa, deeda-e-beena na huwa

(Unless the sea within the drop, the whole within the part
Appear, you play like children; you still lack the seeing eye)

Romance and politics, sensuous lyricism and fiery passion, mingle inextricably in Faiz's poetry. 'The true subject of poetry is loss of the beloved,' he wrote but, in his case, the 'beloved' could mean a lover, country, freedom, even revolution. He had grown up in the intellectual ferment after World War I, the wave of romanticism, the hopes of the October revolution, the emergence of a working class, the stirrings of nationalism. He had seen economic hardship, sleeping often on an empty stomach.

It was inevitable that social realism changed his poetic vision from the purely romantic and he became a founding member of the Progressive Writers' Association. This transformation is best encapsulated by the famous *Mujhse pehli si mohabbat mere mehboob na mang* (Love, do not ask for that love again) in which he goes on to say 'our world knows other torments than of love, and other happiness than a fond embrace.'

Incidentally, after listening to Noor Jehan sing this ghazal, Faiz immediately gifted it to her and thereafter would not even recite it, saying that it belonged to her.

After the Partition of the subcontinent, after what he called the 'pockmarked light' of Independence, after 'the dawn stung by the night', he became the editor of *Pakistan Times* in Lahore but was soon imprisoned in the Rawalpindi Conspiracy case.

Prison walls could not contain the fire in his heart and mind:

Maata-e-loh-o-qalam chhin gayi to kya ghum hai
Ke khun-e-dil mein dubo li hain ungliyan maine
Zuban pe muhar lagi hai to kya rakh di hai
Har ek halqa-e-zanjeer mein zubaan maine

(If ink and pen are snatched from me, shall I
Who have dipped my finger in my heart's blood complain?
Or if they seal my tongue, when I have made
A mouth of every round link of my chain)

The five years in prison, besides adding glamour to his persona, produced some of his best poetry, in praise of freedom, in sympathy with the oppressed of the world, as he felt the restless breeze go past his prison and wondered what havoc had been wrought in the garden beyond:

Chaman mein ghaarat-e-gulchin se jaane kya guzri
Qafas se aaj saba beqaraar guzri hai

Faiz's writing method would be of interest to any writer. Here it is in his own words: 'I do not really know how one writes. Sometimes while reading a book, a phrase or a sentence or an image or a rhyme sticks in the mind, and ultimately, ends up in a poem. At times, while listening to music, a certain note or a certain rhythmic pattern leaves a deep impression. A ghazal first requires the emergence of a rhyming scheme in one's consciousness. One builds on it. For a nazm, one has to think. A line comes first and then you think of the pattern of the poem. It is like an artisan at work. It has to be built. You have to get it into focus. The basic image must be in sharp focus. You have to match things. The music has to be right. No false notes.'

And there were none.

Of the Inconstant Heart

Three weeks to read two hundred-some pages, but that's the kind of book it is. *The Good Soldier—A Tale of Passion* by Ford Madox Ford has the unhurried cadence of the beginning of the twentieth century when readers could indulge themselves, say on a ship journey, reading on the deck all afternoon before it was time to go down to their cabins, open their steamer trunks and dress for dinner. But let me not give you the impression that it is one of those placid books, a tale of idyllic romance or generational family feuds. It is a true tale of passion, a headlong dive into the mysterious depths of the human heart, layered with contradictions, riven with inconstancies.

A few crucial words about the author: Born Ford Hermann Heuffer, Ford produced a large number of books of all sorts (he described himself as 'mad about writing') and edited literary magazines that supported the work of writers like his friend Joseph Conrad, Thomas Hardy, and James Joyce. It was on his fortieth birthday in 1913 that he started *The Good Soldier* 'to show what I could do', intending it to be his last book. And show them he did, producing a classic that has often been described as a perfect novel, a masterpiece of a narrative in which every sentence needs to be read twice to check for hidden traps, insinuations, hints and deceptions. In his personal life, Ford was indecisive and emotionally complicated. While his wife refused to grant him a divorce, he lurched from one love affair to another—the novelist Violet Hunt was followed by the painter Stella Bowen and then by the writer Jean Rhys. His fickle nature and unreliability in matters of the heart clearly seeped into *The Good Soldier*.

At first sight the story is simple enough: The American narrator, Dowell, and his wife Florence meet another wealthy English couple—Edward and Leonora—who are so obviously 'good people'—at a German spa and strike up a close friendship. Their 'intimacy was like a minuet, simply because on every possible occasion and in every possible circumstance we knew where to go, where to sit, which table we unanimously should choose ...' Florence and Edward are both supposedly suffering from weak hearts. When finally they both die not, as we learn later, from their so-called weak hearts but by committing suicide, Dowell is told by Leonora, who has known all along, that the two had an affair for nine long years. Dowell then begins to unravel the whole wretched reality, almost reluctantly, as if he would rather not know. His intention is to do it calmly, as if he is 'at one side of the fireplace of a country cottage, with a sympathetic soul' opposite him. But very soon he begins to bumble as the facts seem to come upon him even as he tells the story. The graceful surface cracks open and out pours all the slime of deception. Good graces hide terrible hatreds, relationships are blackmail, love is a lie and sentiment is just selfishness. His wife never really had a weak heart; she invented it to keep him from the marital bed since day one, reducing him to a lifelong nurse. The perfectly social English couple hasn't spoken to each other in private for years. The good soldier, Edward, appears to the naïve Dowell as 'a hardworking, sentimental and efficient professional man' and seems to approach each of his many love affairs with a deep passion and duty, but is actually quite merciless in these matters. And his cold and seemingly 'normal' wife, when she finds she has finally lost him forever, pushes him over the edge so that he cuts his own throat with a small penknife.

Dowell is the epitome of 'the unreliable narrator' in fiction. He keeps to no chronology. He rushes back and forth over time and place as memories assail him or as revelations occur, leaving in his wake an 'intricate tangle of references and cross-references' as he tells the 'saddest story I have ever heard'. But this is not something he has 'heard' (though Ford maintained that it was indeed something he had heard)—it is a huge deception that he has actually lived through. And ultimately one realizes that the narrator is confused, lost, torn and bleeding. ('I don't know. I know nothing. I am very tired.') Still unable to put blame where it belongs, he concludes that the 'passionate, the headstrong and the too truthful are condemned to suicide and madness' while the 'normal, the virtuous and the slightly deceitful' can flourish.

And towards the end of this carefully constructed though seemingly confused dark tale of human passions emerges the plaintive plea that seems to be as much the narrator's as that of Ford himself: 'Is there any terrestrial paradise where amidst the whispering of the olive leaves, people can be with whom they like and take their ease in shadows and in coolness? Or are all men's lives like the lives of us good people ... broken, tumultuous, agonized, and unromantic lives, periods punctuated by screams, by imbecilities, by deaths, by agonies? Who the devil knows?'

Rainy Day Stories

The wind has been blowing all night, blowing in from the sea with some devilish intent, whistling in wild triumph as it reaches the land. The clay tiles on the roofs of the beach houses clutter in fright and the trees—the straight palms and the strong ficus—bend at the waist. Even the broad brush of the olive, standing on its strong, ancient trunk, sways wildly, out of control. The early-morning sun has no sobering effect. The blue roaring water is flecked right till the horizon with white foam and the beach has been swallowed up. It will continue to blow like this all day, the forecasts say, and perhaps even tomorrow. Only the sun will come and go, giving its place to a grey darkness, which will only deepen the blue of the sea. A day to stay in, a merciful day when all else except the call of books can be put off.

But not any kind of book will do. So I move away the pile of books on history and politics into which I have been dipping like some moody swallow dips into the surface of a summer sea and reach once again for the 1925 collection of Hemingway's stories, *In Our Time*, which contains the short story that best encapsulates what is happening outside my window: 'The Three Day Blow'. It's a relatively short story, told almost entirely as a conversation between Nick Adams (the young protagonist of many of Hemingway's stories) and his friend Bill. The conversation takes place in Bill's house while a foul three-day wind is blowing outside. The two men sit by a roaring fire and start to drink, first finishing a bottle of Irish whiskey that Bill's dad has left and then getting onto another bottle of Scotch that is lying open. Evidently, Bill's dad does not mind drinking as long as it is from a bottle that is already open—it's the opening of bottles that, according to him, makes alcoholics.

And as they drink—with the intention of getting drunk—they talk. It's typical man talk, made even more so by Hemingway's characteristic terseness—of baseball, of Bill's dad, of drinking, of books and writers, including Horace Walpole and G.K. Chesterton. And then finally of Marge, the girl with whom Nick has just broken up. Hemingway readers will recall the prequel to this story, 'The End of Something', in which Nick tells Marjorie, as they are out fishing on the beach at night, that it isn't fun to be with her anymore and their love is done. In that story too, after Marjorie has walked away Bill appears, asking Nick how it went, showing that he was privy to Nick's intent all along, and perhaps even encouraged it. Now, while the wind blows and the whiskey goes home, Bill tells Nick that he did the right thing in throwing Marge over. 'It was the only thing to do. If you hadn't by now you would have been back home working, trying to get enough money to get married ...

Once a man's married he's absolutely bitched. He hasn't got anything more. Nothing. Not a damn thing. He's done for ... They get this sort of fat married look.' But the more Bill tries to justify the decision, the more alone Nick begins to feel. The alcohol leaves his head. 'All he knew was that he had once had Marjorie and that he had lost her. She was gone and he had sent her away. That was all that mattered. He might never see her again. Probably he never would. It was all gone, finished.' All blown away, like the leaves off the trees by the ferocious wind outside.

Then deftly, with each sentence straining on a tight leash, Hemingway changes the nuance. When Bill mentions the danger of renewal of the relationship, Nick sees in that possibility a hope and it's not important to get drunk anymore. They are suddenly out in the cold, shotguns in their hands with Nick revelling in masculine freedom and camaraderie while nursing the hope of renewing a relationship with a woman. 'None of it was important now. The wind blew it out of his head. Still he could always go into town Saturday night. It was a good thing to have in reserve.' This final note that underlines the lack of finality opens up all possibilities.

The thick raindrops are making dull flat sounds on my window panes and joyous hailstones are bouncing off the concrete garden path. It will not stop blowing; on the other hand, it just might.

Go East, Young Man

The Razor's Edge by Somerset Maugham has sold millions of copies in many formats—hardback, paperback, classic; at least two movies have been made on it. But recently I was gifted again the edition that I have always regarded as the original, rightly or wrongly, since it lay for years amongst my father's books, along with Dale Carnegie's *How to Win Friends and Influence People* and Emile Zola's *Nana*.

It's the pocketbook edition with the edges of the pages stained ruby-red and the cover picture of a clean-cut, brilliantined American hero holding up the expectant face of a wavy-haired, equally American heroine against an inky blue, star-filled sky. So once again—after more than three decades—I was away on the same journey, following through the observant and perceptive eyes of Maugham, the spiritual voyage of an American pilot, Larry Darrell, as he searches for meaning in a post-war world and ends up finding it in India.

It wasn't till I was at least thirty pages into the novel (Maugham: 'If I call it a novel it is only because I don't know what else to call it.') that I realized what was happening to

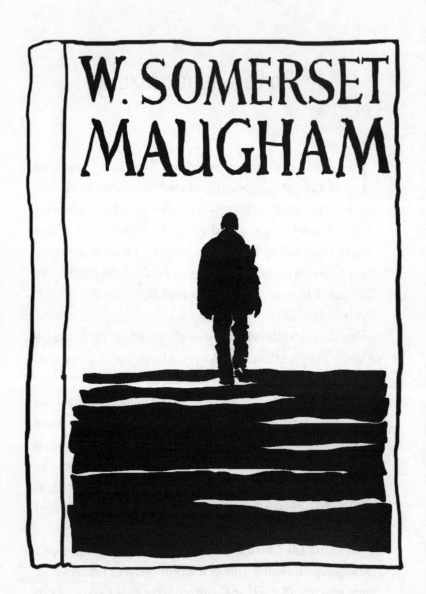

W. SOMERSET MAUGHAM

me. I was having to pace down my mind as I read. The book was unlike any other novel I had read in recent years. It was not a novel in a hurry, tumbling over its own verbal gymnastics, nor was it a flurry of different voices telling the tale from different viewpoints.

This was a story which the writer would tell in his own time. There would be asides and walks along byways, there would be conjecture and speculation. And if the reader was in a hurry, he would only run into a closed door again and again.

So I took several deep breaths, added another pillow and let myself be taken in hand by the narrator, in this case Maugham himself, as he weaved in and out of the story of the main characters, describing their lives and interactions over several years and ending, as he says, 'neither with a death nor a marriage'.

There is the fabulously detailed Elliot Templeton, the society man par excellence till his dying day; the beautiful but limited Isabel and her steady, unromantic husband; the unfortunate and doomed Sophie as she turns from poet to drunken libertine, and Larry himself, the restless soul, seeking Knowledge and the meaning of God and life. There are detailed leisurely descriptions of Paris in all its vagrant and seductive moods. There is observation and perceptiveness in the narration that only Maugham is capable of; there is sympathy and kindliness as well as the inevitable rapier thrust. ('American women expect to find in their husbands a perfection that English women only hope to find in their butlers.')

The heart of the book is tucked towards its end, in a night-long conversation between Larry and Maugham as Larry details his travels in India, his stay at an ashram, his discovery of a guru and his attainment of self-knowledge at an ecstatic moment.

Reams have been written about who the real Larry was. Did Maugham base his story on an American engineer named Guy Hague, whom he could have met at the ashram of Ramana Maharishi when he visited India in 1938? Did he base the story on a chance conversation in 1919 when a young man at a party told him that he wanted to do something interesting with his life? Was the story written many times in earlier attempts, even before Maugham came to India? Did Maugham actually faint when he entered the Maharishi's presence or was it simply the heat?

Naipaul, in his *Half a Life*, has parodied (but surely that must go to Maugham's credit?) the westerner's adventure with eastern spirituality. Nevertheless, it is worth remembering that the book was prescient in this aspect. It was written in 1944, before the beatniks started playing around with dharma, or the Beatles found the Maharishi in Rishikesh or the flower children swayed to Ravi Shankar's sitar.

Before all that, Maugham saw that one day the West, traumatized, exhausted, over-indulged, may come seeking the East. So he wrote this exquisite novel and chose for its epigraph a verse from the Katha Upanishad:

The sharp edge of a razor is difficult to pass over;
Thus the wise say the path to Salvation is hard.

Midnight Musings

It is late at night and I find myself in the tiled and polished anonymity of the waiting room at the Old Delhi Railway station. I am suddenly alone and unexpectedly footloose. My bag is cramped with several half-read books. There is the fascinating tale of the eunuch detective uncovering conspiracies in mist-laden nineteenth-century Istanbul of the Ottomans. It jostles for space with a new book on Sufism with impressively ornate calligraphic illustrations. A murder mystery in modern India written by a young lawyer cries for attention as it pushes against a haunting depiction of a marriage going adrift in the warm and magical light of Jerusalem, way back in the fifties. I could, if I so wished, write about all, or any of them.

But the present is too much with me. The complexities and absurdities of life, its sudden beauty and its lingering pain, its constant surprises, its vanities and its forgetfulness sometimes turn the most exciting fiction into a mere faint shadow.

At such times, it does not appear worthwhile to try and discipline the mind. So, relishing the indifference of strangers around me, I leave the bag of books unopened and let the journey take hold.

The city that I am leaving, though only for a few days, is an old friend, perhaps even an old lover. She and I both know how life has changed the other. There is no need of words, so we let them drop, all the taunts, the pointed complaint, the sly innuendo. Her new fancies stare me in the face. I notice her love of brick and mortar, of steel and glass; I rue her fascination with glitter. I watch her flaunt, with an imperial sweep of her overly bejewelled hand, her soaring new flyovers, the rising stadiums, her shiny new metro, her crazily crafted road corridors, her multiplexes and malls. And I shield myself against the callousness with which she has rejected so much that we once shared—my flower-laden roundabouts, my little theatre café, my corner shop and even my favourite bookshop, owned by a man who knew his books.

Yet there are moments when all does not appear lost. Occasionally, we still exchange glances that no one else can understand. Every once in a while we smile, for no apparent reason, at the same word and on some nights I can even see her tapping her foot though she knows full well that I can only sing out of tune.

On other evenings, we watch as the red dying sun, with merciless disdain, makes equally sharp silhouettes of the mighty Qutub and kikar branches alike. On such evenings she lets her veil slip, ever so tantalizingly. I watch, sipping from my cup of nostalgia, and I see the blaze of the young gulmohars, protected with brick guards along the streets of south Delhi where the houses are still to come up. I see the cascading garlands of yellow amaltas flowers under which a man in pyjamas sells Carryhome ice cream from a pushcart. I see school children buying ice dollies through barbed-wire fences and running back to class even as the syrup drips down their wrists. And all around there are green parks among the single-storeyed houses where groups of boys are playing cricket, French cricket, dog ball cricket, one-tip-catch-out cricket. There is even a glimpse of college students in woollen dressing gowns warming their hands on a coal fire some faraway December, waiting for the tea to boil in a blackened saucepan. And from somewhere there rises, along with the full moon, a full-throated ghazal against the backdrop of Mughal ruins. There is so much else too that need not, cannot, go into words. The blood knows. We both know. And we let it be.

For the cities that we truly love are the cities of our minds, lying in the cradle of childhood or on the crest of youth. Each one is a personal Shangri La which age cannot wither, beyond the tick-tock of time. And ever so often we return to them, searching for the light that has not faded, the companions who have not aged, the idealism that has not soured.

Finally, an hour behind time, the train begins to move, leaving behind the platform shrouded in surreal bluish white light. We will not cross the river tonight but that does not matter. Whatever the direction, there is only the dark night that stretches beyond the city. And I know what awaits me at the straggling colonial railway station at Kalka, which I will reach in time for the first call of the day by the local muezzin. There, once the last stars have faded, will be the comfortable silhouettes of the freshly bathed hills, the balm of the mist as it will rise to greet me, the certainty that I will fall asleep to the sound of the cicadas, and the birds will come to wake me up.

Obsessions, Destructive
and Redemptive

Every once in a while—sometimes in a very long while—you come across a book that you wish would not finish. You savour each sentence, linger long over each turning page, go back every once in a while and often put the book down to absorb the full meaning of what has just been read. Such was Graham Greene's *The End of an Affair* which I caressed slowly to its last page in a small district town. Such has been *The Great Gatsby* which I end up reading every couple of years and never fail to stumble upon some new and exciting insight. And this time it has been Michael Ondaatje's marvellous poem of a novel, *The English Patient*.

There are several striking aspects of the novel, each deserving an informed essay. The novel's form, for instance: its perspectives shift as quickly and seamlessly as the desert sands it describes and the past intertwines intensely with the present until each moment actually becomes timeless. Or the impact of war on the four fractured lives thrown together in an abandoned and half-destroyed Tuscany villa—the burnt, almost-dead patient Almasy sifting through his still glistening memories, the thumbless thief Caravaggio, the partially shell-shocked nurse Hana and the intensely focused Sikh sapper, Kip. The villa itself, with its overgrown garden, its crucifix working as a scarecrow, its landmines, its locked-up rooms, much like the souls of the characters which open but gradually to reveal their secrets, can be a subject for separate study. As can the artful making of this luminous novel into a searing movie with its haunting imagery and powerful portrayal: Ralph Fiennes is as definitively the English patient as Peter O' Toole is Lawrence of Arabia.

But the book's highlight is Ondaatje's incredible language, the language of a spare miniaturist using the least strokes to create a haunting effect, his pen moving as delicately as Katherine Clifton's paintbrush in the opening scene of the film. Like the time when Caravaggio watches the Italian night settling down around him: 'The noise of trees, the breaking of moon into silver fish bouncing off the leaves of asters outside. The moon is on him like skin, a sheaf of water.' Or his description of the 'deepest sorrow ... Where the only way to survive is to excavate everything.' Or the carelessly strewn bits of throwaway wisdom: 'Birds prefer trees with dead branches. They have complete vistas from where they perch. They can take off in any direction.'

Ondaatje rises to sublime heights when describing the obsessions at the core of the novel, obsessions beyond reason, obsessions both destructive and redemptive. The most powerful passions are transmitted with a few well-chosen words, or even with silences. The obsession of Almasy and his group of explorers with the desert, forever sailing into the past to uncover its buried secrets, searching for the eternal lost oasis. 'In the desert the most loved waters, like a lover's name, are carried blue in your hands, enter your throat. One swallows absence.' Or the obsession of Hana with the English patient, whom she must nurse even when he is beyond nursing. The obsession of Caravaggio to unravel the true identity of the English patient by making him talk, uncaring that the patient will soon be dead, or in a way died already when he fell burning out of the sky.

But the thief must know, even as he shares the patient's morphine to still, for a moment, their shared destiny of intense pain. And Hana's obsession with Kip as she yearns to redeem through love his soul deadened by battle, forever listening for the false step, the crossed wire, the hidden death. Kip's obsession with his profession, his desire to defuse the last possible landmine, to the extent that he cannot even listen to a piano without fearing that it will blow up.

And towering above all, the doomed obsession of Almasy and Katherine, all 'the paranoia and claustrophobia of hidden love,' played out in a shuttered room above the bazaar of imported parrots, in the colonial hallways and in the indigo markets of Cairo. He listens to her with the classical face, reciting poetry across a desert fire, and falls in love with a voice. 'Only a voice. I wanted to hear nothing more.' From then on it is a struggle between betrayal and honour, a plummeting into the desert in a flurry of flames, an obsession with the hollow at the base of a neck, with perspiration on a swerving knee during a long, hot journey. And in the end 'it is not the morality, it is how much you can bear.'

What does one do with a book like that? Except read it again and again.

A Wizard Called Oz

Ramat Aviv is a leafy suburb of Tel Aviv, the understated terrain of the intellectuals, lawyers and professors, politicians and journalists. On the top floor of one of the buildings that face a park in the heart of this sylvan, silent suburb is the apartment where Amos Oz lives, mostly on weekends. He spends most of his days in Arad, a small town at the edge of the desert, overlooking the Dead Sea. It's the desert that provides him the eternal silence that he yearns for every morning, the calm that he tries to distil into his writing. There is no name on the buzzer at the entrance. You have to know where he lives, or you have to guess it. Or you have to be expected.

He is quietly endearing, boyish at seventy, as he opens the door and I stumble in, wrong-footed by the fact that there is no ice to be broken. We talk for a while of nations born of dreams, and the disappointments inherent in the nature of dreams. Then he vanishes to the kitchen to make coffee, leaving me alone in a sea of books.

From the floor to the ceiling, except where the window allows one to kiss the treetops, they lie in rigorous order. Philip Roth, Ruth Prawer Jhabvala, Bruce Chatwin, Ben

Okri ... and translations of Oz in several languages. I am reminded of the scene in his autobiographical *A Tale of Love and Darkness* where the child Amos is given a section of his father's bookshelf to put his books upon and the painful effort that goes into arranging and rearranging those few titles. And of Oz's childhood ambition, fuelled by post-Holocaust fear, to become a book. People, even writers, got killed. But there was always a chance that a copy of a book would survive in some forlorn corner of the world, 'in Reykjavik, Valladolid or Vancouver'.

The author of such masterpieces as *The Black Box*, the man on everybody's shortlist for the Nobel Prize for several years, is soon back with the coffee, in red cups without plates, wiping stray drops with his handkerchief. He talks easily, in smooth formulations, as if too many interviewers have gone down the same path.

'All literature is provincial. It has to have a specific location. International fiction is only to be bought at international airports and left on benches.' Naturally we turn to Faulkner, who urged writers to return to the 'old verities and truths of the heart, the universal truths lacking which any story is ephemeral and doomed—love and honour and pity and pride and compassion and sacrifice'. Oz agrees and adds: 'When I visited Oxford, Mississippi the place was only a poor, fading replica of the fictitious place that appears in Faulkner's novels'.

Glancing at his books in my hands, he comments: 'It's always a living miracle when I meet a reader. A reader is a co-producer of a book. I write the musical score, he plays it. If the reader reads about a sunset, he brings to it all the sunsets he has ever seen. That is why no two readers ever read the same book. You can admire paintings or listen to music and be talking to a friend, but when you read, you read alone. You are part of the process.'

His words bring forth the images of his mother, described in *A Tale of Love and Darkness*, her knees folded under her, bent over a book of Turgenev, Chekhov or Maupassant, reading after a morning of household chores in the damp basement flat, 'surrounded by zinc tubs and pickled gherkins and the geranium that was dying in a rusty

olive drum'. Ultimately, the reading was not escape enough from the tawdriness of provincial, war-torn Jerusalem and she killed herself in 1952, leaving anger and hurt in young Amos. 'Is that the way to leave, rudely, in the middle of a sentence?' Almost unconsciously, a recurring image creeps into many books, of a woman 'who used to spend hours standing at the window, with a glass of tea getting cold in her hand, with her face to the pomegranate bush and her back to the room.'

His words draw me back to the book-filled room: 'You write because you want to tell stories. It's like dreaming or falling in love. You want to tell stories, hear stories since the age of two or three. Stories have been told around Neanderthal fires, stories predate the alphabet.'

After his mother's death, Oz went to live in a kibbutz, in the manner of the bronzed and broad-shouldered pioneers, the revolutionary worker poets, whom he had long idealized. There he alternated between working in the fields and scribbling stories. '*My Michael* was written in the bathroom when I was twenty-four. I then thought I knew all about women and could write like a woman. I would not dare to do it today. I wanted a free day to write. The kibbutz elders debated it and one of them, an "old man of forty", even said that I may be great writer, perhaps the next Tolstoy, but I needed to work in the fields till I was fifty to learn about life. I got my one day finally, and after my first book of stories and a novel were published, I got two and then four days a week.' All his early royalties went to the kibbutz and it was not till he was forty-six that he actually moved out and opened a bank account. There is a little graveyard near the kibbutz which he is fond of pointing out. 'Most of my characters lie buried there, or bits of many characters.' People whom he knew, who lived, breathed, loved and cheated. For nothing is pure fiction.

Evenly and unhurriedly he talks some more about writing. 'It took me five years to write *The Same Sea*. I wanted to remove the boundaries between prose and poetry, between fiction and faction, between music and writing. I wanted to make the pages dance and sing, even leaving sentences half finished on the page.' I pick up the marvellous product of that effort and request him to sign it for me. And then it's time to go. As I leave he modestly informs me: 'Two of my books have been translated into Malayalam.'

Strange and Mystic Business

Allenby Street in Tel Aviv is a busy place at lunch time. Amidst the roadside cafés, the pizzerias, the shop fronts full of mannequins in shiny dresses and corner boutiques where people seem to be forever buying sunglasses, one can easily miss a half-open gate with its small board pointing the way to Halpers, one of the several second-hand bookshops on Allenby. But once inside, time is put on hold.

There are rows of floor-to-ceiling shelves creaking with the weight of old books, there is jazz in the background and below the skin, there is the excitement of a huge and thrilling discovery. Sobriety returns in about half an hour: the shop is there to stay, there will be more visits. So for the moment, four yellowing, sweet-smelling books are enough. And of the four, it's John Steinbeck's *Journal of a Novel*, with its crumbling, fragile pages that I first open.

'Dear Pat: How did the time pass and how did it grow so late.' With these elegiac words, Steinbeck began this *Journal*, in the form of letters to his good friend and editor, Pascal 'Pat' Covici, as an accompaniment to the first draft of his novel *East of Eden*. Written from January through

November 1951, there is a letter for each day spent working on the novel.

In fact the letters were written on the left-hand-side pages of the large format notebook, on the right-hand side of which Steinbeck was writing his book. In the end, it stood as an independent literary achievement, never intended for publication but eloquent about Steinbeck's emotional condition—he was comfortably settled into a New York apartment with his third wife, recovering from the death of his best friend and from a divorce—as well as his working methods and commitment to his writing.

Most importantly, *Journal of a Novel* provides an honest and open view of how Steinbeck visualized, planned and executed what he believed was his biggest book in which he was determined to use 'every form, every method, every technique' that he had honed. All that had come before was regarded as only practice for this book. Set in his native Salinas Valley of California, *Eden* would be the classic retelling of the Cain and Abel story, 'the story of good and evil, of strength and weakness, of love and hate, of beauty and ugliness ...' He decided to write the story as if addressing his two young sons, to ensure simplicity and directness, and because he felt that unless he told them, they would never know what they came from.

And he felt prepared. 'All the experiment is over now. I either write the book or I do not. There can be no excuses ... This book will be the most difficult of all I have ever attempted. Whether I am good enough or gifted enough remains to be seen. I do have a good background. I have love and I have had pain. I still have anger but I can find no bitterness in myself ... I think perhaps it is the only book that I have ever written. I think there is only one book to a man.'

And this from a man who had written *The Grapes of Wrath* thirteen years earlier; *The Winter of Our Discontent* and the Nobel Prize were still a decade away. *Journal of a Novel*, used by Steinbeck as a warming up for the daily work on the novel, also provides a fascinating view of a novelist at work. Uphill and alone most of the time, trudging through an uncertain landscape, clinging only to some momentary vision glimpsed through the mists of his mind, waiting for the downhill rush that may or may not come.

Like most writers, Steinbeck fears the putting down of the first line. 'It is amazing the terrors, the magics, the prayers, the straightening shyness that assails me ... A strange and mystic business, writing.' One feels his quiet resolve, reserving the first part of every day for the book, out of 'a necessary selfishness—otherwise books do not get written'. Doggedly and unhurriedly he lets the story unfold through the 'slow, leisurely pyramiding of detail'. There are the good days and bad days—'some days smile and others have thin slitted eyes ...'

And there are the sheer eccentricities of the craftsman: He wrote in soft, black pencil which had to be a certain length and worried constantly about having a dozen of the right ones at hand, perfectly sharpened. By the time the first draft of 350,000 words was done, he had gone through twenty-five dozen of them and had a callus on his writing finger that he had to sandpaper down. He found relief in crafting wooden objects on his carpenter's bench, including a paperweight that could stand on an inclining desk. The sleeplessness, the nightingale in his workroom and a hundred other such details ... *Journal of a Novel* is essential reading for anybody struggling with the desire to write, anybody brave enough to try, as Steinbeck says, 'in utter loneliness ... to explain the inexplicable'.

No Game for Knights

'The most durable thing in writing is style and style is the
most important investment a writer can make with
his time,' said novelist Raymond Chandler, and certainly
he practised what he preached. His 1939 novel *The Big
Sleep*, the first—though certainly not the last—of his that
I read is so steeped in style that it crackles. Having tried
his hand, with varying degrees of lack of success, at the
civil service, journalism, stringing tennis racquets, picking
fruit and book-keeping, Chandler turned to writing private
detective stories for pulp magazines and after six years of
maturing produced *The Big Sleep*. With that he created the
archetypal private detective in Philip Marlowe, who along
with Dashiell Hammett's Sam Spade, has defined all private
detectives produced in fiction since. All the cool, laconic,
tough men with an often surprising sense of right and
wrong; to the extent that even Ian Fleming can be counted
among his admirers.

Set in Los Angeles of the 1930s, *The Big Sleep* depicts a
dark and uncertain world, a world of pornographers and
gamblers, operating under the protective eye of crooked
law officers, a world of blackmail, double-crossing and

killing. And, of course, blondes. (A famous Chandler quote: 'I do a lot of research—particularly in the apartments of tall blondes.') A corrupt, morally decayed world where love rings hollow and glamour only hides ugliness. Into such a world steps the 'painfully' honest, hard-boiled private detective Philip Marlowe, with his eagle eye and somewhat anachronistic sense of ethics.

We know him from the first paragraph on: 'I was wearing my powder-blue suit, with dark blue shirt, tie and display handkerchief, black brogues, black wool socks with dark blue clocks on them. I was neat, clean, shaved and sober, and I didn't care who knew it. I was everything the well-dressed private detective ought to be. I was calling on four million dollars.' Though very unlike 'the greasy little men snooping around hotels' who usually typify private detectives, Marlowe soon gets rid of the powder-blue suit and pulls on his trench-coat to investigate the blackmail case handed over to him. He dashes off to the nearest drugstore to buy a pint of whisky and uses enough of it to keep him 'warm and interested'. He does so in his own style and manner and as he tells the tall elder daughter— the fleeting romantic interest—of the man who hires him: 'I don't mind if you don't like my manners. They're pretty bad. I grieve over them during the long winter evenings.'

By the time the book ends, Marlowe seems out of his depth in a world that has lost all moorings of morality. To the dead men around him, he says: 'You just slept the big sleep, not caring about the nastiness of how you died or where you fell. Me, I was part of the nastiness now.' In fact, the realisation of how outdated his ethics are had come to him earlier when in a prize scene he continues to stare at his chessboard even as the young blonde is trying to seduce him. 'The move with the knight was wrong ... Knights had no meaning in this game. It wasn't a game for knights.'

As one turns the pages of *The Big Sleep*, one would be forgiven for thinking that one is in an old-fashioned theatre, watching a black-and-white Hollywood movie, with scene after scene of rain-swept night streets, winged-tail Chevrolets, tough men in Fedoras, cigarettes hanging limply from the corners of their lips, dinner-jacketed gamblers and long-legged femme fatales in black dresses ... Written in three months, the book seems to have internalized the fast pace of its writer, heightened by its taut and fast dialogue, full of rapier thrusts worthy of a Cyrano.

Clearly, it was a book made for a movie and Phil Marlowe's was a role begging to be played by Humphrey Bogart. It all duly happened in 1946 when Bogart's trench-coated casual masculinity crashed with devastating effect with the delectable blonde look of Lauren Bacall. The screenplay was written by, among others, none other than William Faulkner.

The style element of *The Big Sleep* comes, firstly, from the icy cool voice of the narrator and then largely from the use of language. With amazing ease, Chandler strews similes and one-liners across the pages until it begins to seem completely natural. The first blonde who enters the book is seen to have 'little sharp predatory teeth, as white as fresh orange pith and as shiny as porcelain'. She is the same one whose face falls 'apart like a bride's pie crust' and into whose eyes, when he brushes aside her literally naked advances, doubt creeps in 'noiselessly, like a cat in long grass stalking a young blackbird'. Plants have stalks 'like the newly washed fingers of dead men' and dry white hairs cling to the scalp of an old man 'like wild flowers fighting for life on a bare rock'.

The same old man, weak and dying, uses 'his strength as carefully as an out-of-work showgirl uses her last good pair of stockings'. Bubbles rise in a glass 'like false hopes', the lady's 'breath is as delicate as the eyes of a fawn' and blood begins to move around in him 'like a prospective tenant looking over a house'.

And I have saved some of my favourite one-liners for the end. First: 'She was as sore as an alderman with the mumps'; two: 'It seemed like a nice neighbourhood to have bad habits in', and three: 'Dead men are heavier than broken hearts'.

In the Twilight Zone with Coetzee

I have just read two books by J.M. Coetzee in quick succession and I wonder how long it will be before I can pick up a book by another author and not fling it away as meaningless. I know that I will recover and the spell that Coetzee has created will pass; in time the whirlwind will die down, the mind will stop trying to hold on to phantom images floating in the half-light or to find rational answers to questions that are not meant to have any answers.

But for the moment, I drift with Coetzee in the twilight zone—somewhere between life and death, between the known and the unknown, between certainty and doubt.

In the first of the two books, *The Master of Petersburg*, one is led there by none other than Dostoevsky himself, who has, in this imagined episode, been called back to Petersburg from Dresden by the death of his stepson. Petersburg was never just another city to Russian writers. Gogol portrayed it as the capital of alienation, illusion and deception in his soul-crushing *Tales of Petersburg*, a city where human greed and vanity ruled supreme. And Dostoevsky added a dimension of fantasy to the city. In the fevered imagination of his characters, it became a fog-bound city of hallucinations, visions and dreams; its long summer daylight could not only enchant but also play havoc on sleepless minds and tortured nerves.

In Coetzee's novel, the ghostly visions of this city are always at hand as Dostoevsky struggles to come to terms with the death of his stepson, in the process entering headlong into unexpected political intrigue and conflict. He takes over the room where his son lodged and forges ambiguous relationships with the landlady and her young daughter, to whom his son was not just a lodger but a hero, a revolutionary in the making, a man recovering from a lost childhood, even from a selfish stepfather.

In that room he struggles with his son's memory, his visions and his smells, his ambitions and regrets, trying almost to will him back to life; in that room, too, his grief duels with his passion, in a doomed liaison with the landlady.

Soon he discovers that his son had joined the anarchists and now the arch anarchist, Nechaev, disguised as a woman, is trying to tempt him into the same game. Will he lend his writing, his respectable name, to their movement? Will he join them as they try to create a new future by destroying all that is old? Or will he continue to wallow in political apathy, writing about Russia's miseries? The anarchists obviously rest their hope on the fact that in reality Dostoevsky was arrested for being part of a radical group and was saved from the firing squad by a last-minute reprieve.

As he plods his melancholy way around the city, forever in fear of his next epileptic fit, the Master struggles too with his inner demons, his fickle dark desires, his split loyalties. 'This is not the lodging house of madness in which he is living, nor is Petersburg a city of madness. He is the mad one; and the one who admits he is the mad one is mad too. Nothing he says is true, nothing is false, nothing is to be trusted, nothing to be dismissed. There is nothing to hold to, nothing to do but fall.'

Not an easy book by any means, not one that lends itself to clear resolutions, and even the plot that seems to form does so only to vanish again, like a midnight vision over the Neva. The only redemption seems to lie in the act of writing: '... he experiences, today, an exceptional sensual pleasure—in the feel of the pen, snug in the crook of his thumb, but even more in the feel of his hand being tugged back lightly from its course across the page by the strict, unvarying shape of the letters, the discipline of the alphabet.'

Waiting for the Barbarians is an earlier book, not quite as spare and monastic as Coetzee's later work, but as bleak and unrelenting in its assessment of the human condition.

The setting is unnamed: some say it is a backwater of apartheid South Africa, others believe, because of the descriptions of snow, that it is Central Asia. It is in any case a frontier, the zone between the known and the feared unknown, the so-called civilized and the barbaric. There the unnamed Magistrate, a likeable, liberal, humanistic civil servant, spends his days, enjoying his siestas and his concubines, at peace with his surroundings.

Until the Empire that he is supposed to represent comes upon him, desperate in its dying throes to put all enemies, supposed or real, to the sword. And the proud, ambitious representatives of the empire, the merchants of torture, do not trust men like the Magistrate. Condemned for his supposed softness towards the so-called barbarians, evidenced by his strange desire for a prisoner girl nearly blinded by torture, he is brutalized, demeaned and broken. And yet, there is something, some strand of humanity, which cannot be broken, even though all fancy ideas of justice are blown out of his mind by inhuman torture.

Two very strange and powerful books then from a man who, in the words of Bernard Levin, 'sees the heart of darkness in all societies, and gradually it becomes clear that he is not dealing in politics at all, but inquiring into the nature of the beast that lurks within each of us'.

The Guest from the Future

Things left half done tend to nag. Earlier, I recounted the meetings of Isaiah Berlin with Boris Pasternak but left for another time the story of his dramatic night-long conversation with the poetess Anna Akhmatova which she, with some artistic exaggeration, identified as the cause of the Cold War. To set matters at rest, I turned to the biography, *Anna Akhmatova: Poet and Prophet*, by Roberta Reeder.

Berlin enters the scene only on Page 286, more than half way through. Akhmatova was in her mid-fifties, having been born in 1889, in the twilight of Imperial Russia. She had already been the toast of literary Petersburg to the extent that she appears as a defining detail in a contemporary memoir of the city: 'Fog, streets, bronze horses, triumphal arches over the gates, Akhmatova, sailors and academics, the Neva, railings, murmuring lines at the bread shops, stray bullets of light from broken street lamps have settled in my memory ... of the past, like love, like a disease, like the years.'

She had also been condemned as a 'half nun, half harlot' after the revolution and regarded as a relic of a bygone corrupt age, a selfish poetess obsessed with personal feelings and not sufficiently starry-eyed about the revolution. *The Literary Encyclopaedia of 1929* described her as 'a poetess of the aristocracy who has not found a new function in capitalist society, but has already lost her old function in feudal society'. She was not permitted to publish for fifteen years until one day in 1939 Stalin asked: 'Where is Akhmatova? Why isn't she writing?' Evidently, her collection *From Six Books* was allowed to come out because Stalin's daughter loved her poetry; the book was nicknamed 'Papa's gift to Svetlana'.

Akhmatova had already loved, and been loved by, many men, including the painter Modigliani, then unknown and poor. Together, they walked the streets of Paris in the moonlight and he drew her enigmatic features. As she wrote, the relationship was a turning point in their artistic lives: 'Everything that had happened to us up until that point was the prehistory of our lives ... it was the hour just before the dawn.' She had also seen many loved ones become victims to Stalinist terror in the years of the dreaded midnight knock, including her first husband Gumilyov and the poet Osip Mandelstam.

Browsing in a Leningrad bookstore in the autumn of 1945, Berlin—then functioning as a First Secretary in the British embassy—met the literary scholar, V.N. Orlov. The two went to see Akhmatova the same afternoon. He found her 'immensely dignified, with unhurried gestures, a noble head, beautiful, somewhat severe features, and an expression of immense sadness. Suddenly he heard his name being shouted outside. Below the window stood Winston Churchill's son Randolph, who was visiting Russia as a journalist and, having been told at the bookstore that Berlin had gone to see Akhmatova, had followed him there. Not knowing her apartment, he had resorted to the method of an Oxford undergrad; standing in the courtyard and yelling the name.

Berlin left quickly with him, knowing how dangerous it was for a Soviet citizen to meet with a foreigner even privately, let alone having Churchill's son shouting in the garden below. He went back later to see Akhmatova and they talked through the night of Russian literature, common friends, her loneliness and isolation. He noted that she spoke without self-pity, 'like a princess in exile, proud, unhappy, unapproachable ...' She would write in her cycle of poems, *Cinque*: 'That late night dialogue turned into/The delicate shimmer of interlaced rainbows.'

Rumours began to circulate because of Randolph's presence that a foreign delegation had come to take Akhmatova away and Churchill would send a special plane for her. Word reached Stalin, who said: 'This means our nun is now receiving visits from foreign spies.' Berlin visited her again in January 1946 and the day after, a microphone was screwed into her ceiling. That summer Akhmatova was denounced by the Central Committee of the Party and expelled from the Writers Union. The Leningrad Party Secretary, Zhdanov, attacked her for her 'gloomy tones of hopelessness before death, mystic experiences intermingled with eroticism … a harlot-nun whose sin is mixed with prayer'. More attacks followed and her son was arrested in 1949. Once again she began to burn her poetry after committing it to memory.

Isaiah Berlin returned to Russia in 1956. Fearing another arrest of her son, she refused to meet the man who had been the subject of some of her most beautiful love poems. He spoke to her on the phone and also gave her the news of his recent marriage. He describes her reaction: "'I see.' There followed a long silence. "I am sorry you cannot see me, Pasternak says your wife is charming." Another long silence'.

Her strong attraction to Berlin and its distillation into poetry had many reasons: He had grown up in Russia before going abroad and could relate to her suffering. His analytical mind, keen perception and wide knowledge made him a kindred soul with the sensitivity and intellect to understand her every nuance. The meeting with him brought out the feelings she had bottled up to avoid rejection: 'And that door that you half opened/I don't have the strength to slam'. But it is these lines from 'A Dream' which best capture the essence of the night-long meeting:

We met in an unbelievable year
When the world's strength was at an ebb,
Everything was in mourning, everything withered by
   adversity,
And only the graves were fresh.
Without streetlights, the Neva's waves were black as
   pitch,
Thick night enclosed me like a wall ...
That's when my voice called out to you!
Why it did—I still don't understand.
And you came to me, as if guided by a star
That tragic autumn, stepping
Into that irrevocably ruined house,
From whence had flown a flock of burnt verse.

96, Not Out

A meeting with a literary icon can sometimes be imbued with excitement akin to that of a lovers' tryst. With a knowing smile, it seems, this thought crosses my mind on tiptoe, as I stand in the smoky, early winter dusk of Sujan Singh Park, glancing repeatedly at my watch. Finally, at seven sharp, I step up to the door that says famously, 'Do Not Ring Unless Expected', and bravely thumb the doorbell knowing that, ninety-six though he may be, Khushwant Singh does not forget his appointments.

It seems that time has bypassed that living room which I enter after a gap of more than two years. The books, the photographs, the drinks table and the author himself on his sofa chair in the corner, wearing a black woollen cap, his legs stretched out on a stool and a rough shawl thrown over them. A closer look shows that he is perhaps frailer than he was two years earlier, and perhaps he needs the hearing aid a bit more, but the sight of the strong drink of whisky that already stands near his right hand is reassuring. He watches carefully, unwilling to begin the conversation, until my drink has been served along with the wasabi-coated peas and butter-drenched fresh mushroom vol-au-vents.

Inevitably, we begin to talk of his latest novel, *The Sunset Club*. He reaches out to a side table and hands me a card for the launch party. 'I was asked to do it when I was ninety-five. I said I am not going to do it, I am too old. But the idea wouldn't go away. So I started writing. You know I am an agnostic, but I call God Bade Mian. I said: Bade Mian, you have to give me one year so that I can complete the novel. When I finished it, I said, Bade Mian, you have to give me six months to see it published. These six months finish on November 30 when the book is being launched. Now I am asking Bade Mian for more time to see how the book does, what the reviewers say.' All along, his fingers hold his forehead in a characteristic gesture and his infectious laughter makes you part of his conspiracy. He and I both know that the book will do very well. The first edition of the recent volume, *Absolute Khushwant*, containing his distilled thoughts on subjects ranging from love to religion, as told to Humra Quraishi, sold out in three days flat.

And does he still write every day? 'Yes, every single day. Actually I wake up at three in the morning and I brood. I feel sorry for myself, I have so many ailments.' His gentle smile and a timely sip of his drink belie that statement. 'Then I get the morning's newspapers and waste my time doing crossword puzzles. Only after my siesta do I begin to write, and continue till the evening. If I don't write every day, it becomes too difficult to start again. The sight of that blank page and the challenge of having to fill it! It gets easier after the first page. I must write three or four

pages every day, otherwise I do not feel I have earned my whisky.' This from a man who cannot remember how many books he has written, only that the list runs into yards. And besides the books there are the two columns every week, now translated into several regional languages, enabling Khushwant Singh to be read by 'chaiwallahs at railway stations, policemen on patrol and butchers in Khan Market'.

An open book of Urdu poetry lies face down near his left hand. I recall an entire section on the subject in *Absolute Khushwant* in which he writes: 'I keep Ghalib on my bedside table and an anthology of Urdu poetry on the table beside me where I sit the entire day.' When I draw his attention to it, he raises his glass and quotes Ghalib:

Goh hath ko jumbish nahin, ankhon mein to dum hai
Rahne do abhi sagar-o-mina mere aage

(Though the hand is powerless, the eye is still alive
Let the jug and goblet remain before me)

And where does he place Faiz Ahmad Faiz in the ranks of Urdu poets? I cannot resist asking. 'Very high,' is his quick answer. 'Faiz was two years my senior in Lahore, at Government College. I met him years later when I went to Pakistan. I went to have breakfast with him and he was drinking whisky. Then I came back for lunch and he was drinking whisky. But he was never drunk. And the other Urdu poet, Ahmad Faraz: when he came to my room to have some whisky, he dipped his cigarette in his drink and said that this way he can enjoy both together!'

All this talk is not wasted on me. I hurry to my second drink; he is only halfway through his only one. I wonder aloud if his evening darbars carry on with their usual regularity. 'Actually I am thinking that I will stop meeting people altogether,' he says. 'I want to sit in the dark and drink my whisky; otherwise, I am not being fair to it.' But I know that he yearns for silence and solitude for other reasons he has written about. 'It is work, my writing that keeps me going. Writing is a solitary profession and you simply cannot write in a crowd or in the midst of people. Over the years I have discovered what enormous energy silence creates, energy that socializing and useless chit-chat depletes. You have got to train yourself to be alone. You have to discipline yourself to follow a slavish routine.'

It is ten to eight and I know I must gracefully depart. Even as he looks meaningfully at my glass, I quickly drain it, toasting his health and his pen, and step out. For some reason I am exuberant and cheerful, unmindful of the traffic. Those who have visited this literary lion in his winter will share the feeling.

A Latin Interlude

When Mario Vargas Llosa, the celebrated Peruvian novelist, entered the casually elegant garden for dinner under a full summer moon, he came from the little gate at the back. There was no momentous entry, no trumpets and drums. Just a casual reach for a glass of red wine and easy conversation with the other big literary names around the table.

These others must wait their turn; we will listen only to him, him with his silvery hair and easy laugh and hearty voice. Before and after that conversation, I have read and re-read *Touchstones*, his brilliant essays on literature, art and politics. I am no longer sure where his voice dies down and the essays pick up, or where the paragraphs fade away and he begins to speak ...

Filtering slowly through the miasma of West Asian and Latin politics, the conversation inches towards what Vargas Llosa calls the 'seeds of dreams', the makings of a writer.

For him, these lie in a large house in Cochabamba in Bolivia where he spent his early years with his grandparents, mother and cousins, listening to stories and sinking happily into mounds of children's fiction and the worlds of Ivanhoe, Tarzan, Sandokan and Captain Nemo.

His father was not there, as Vargas Llosa recalls, standing near that sweet-smelling bush in the garden. He was supposed to be dead; he was only the much-loved photograph of a handsome marine in a uniform. In fact, his parents had divorced and, his mother being Catholic, this was a disgrace and a secret. Finally one day, walking by the river, she told the young Mario that his father was alive. Not only that, the two had secretly remarried. When they met, Mario hated his father. And the latter believed that writing was a lost cause and even an indication that Mario was gay.

It was only when his son's photograph appeared in *Time* Magazine, with all its implicit certification of veracity, that Mario's father took his chosen vocation seriously. Based on his childhood experiences, Vargas Llosa concludes that everything he has written has its roots in lived experience.

'It was something that I saw, heard, but also read, that my memory retained with a singular and mysterious stubbornness, that formed certain images which, sooner or later, and for reasons that I also find very difficult to fathom, became a stimulus for fantasy, a starting point for a complete imaginary construction.'

The Time of the Hero came from his days at the Military Academy; a trip to the Upper Maranon gave the material for *The Green House*, as did the solitary brothel in the Peruvian city of Piura, and *The Way to Paradise*, a tale about the painter Gauguin and his grandmother, involved travel to the South Sea islands.

Lived experience aside, Vargas Llosa believes that every writer is essentially a reader and admits the influence of all he has read: Sartre's ideas on committed writing, or the epic style of Malraux or the American twentieth century greats: Hemingway, Fitzgerald, Steinbeck, Dos Passos.

But William Faulkner, he says as he turns to carefully sign a book, was the greatest influence on all Latin American writers. From Faulkner, he learnt the prime importance of form in fiction and the infinite possibilities offered by point-of-view and the construction of time in a story.

'Without the wonderment that I felt when I discovered the richness of shades, allusions, perspectives, harmonies and ambiguities of his prose, and the absolutely original way in which he organized his stories, I would never have dared to rearrange "real" narrative chronology in my own work, or to present an episode from different points of view and levels of reality ...' Faulkner's master, he believes, was James Joyce, as evidenced by the form of *Ulysses*; it's heartening to learn that Vargas Llosa too, like most of us, could not finish *Finnegans Wake*.

The same issues of the narrative point of view and time in fiction are also examined in an essay on Don Quixote. 'Even if they do not know it, contemporary novelists who play with form, distort time, mix up different points of view and experiment with language, are all indebted to Cervantes.'

The complexities of narration also form the greatest strength of Virginia Woolf's *Mrs Dalloway*. 'Only failed fictions reproduce reality: successful fictions abolish and transfigure reality,' he writes. The readers of *Mrs Dalloway* never confront an objective reality but a subjective version woven by the narrators in which life is transformed into 'memory, feeling, sensation, desire, impulse ...'

Mrs Dalloway also, incidentally, greatly influenced the other towering Latin writer, Gabriel Garcia Marquez. I ask Vargas Llosa whether he can think of any other way in which *A Hundred Years of Solitude* could have been written. He says that it is very difficult to say, praising Marquez for the way in which he so seamlessly wove together a century, the lives and events of a bygone era.

I cannot resist asking him whether it is true that the two writers have not spoken since 1976 when their friendship ended in a spat and he allegedly gave Marquez a black eye. With a winning smile, he denies comment and turns the conversation to India. He talks of Kipling and Kim's cannon—the Zamzama—that now stands outside the Lahore museum, of Octavio Paz and of Pablo Neruda's poems of India.

And suddenly, with the moon now overhead, he begins to recite in Spanish, Neruda's immortal lines—Tonight I can write the saddest lines./I loved her, and sometimes she loved me too—lines that everybody in Latin America once knew by heart.

I no longer have the heart to write about his politics or the time he ran for the Peruvian Presidency and read fiction only at five in the morning. Neruda's lines have touched too many strings, opened up too many veins.

Come with Old Khayyam

The other day, halfway through a virtual conversation, or chat, I found myself unable to recall a much loved rubai of Omar Khayyam. This lapse, unimaginable in one's youth but part of the daily landscape now, soon had me searching the bookshelves. I was looking for my Omar Khayyam and, unconsciously, I was looking for that coverless, disintegrating Jaico edition I had bought in the mid-1970s for two or three rupees from the booksellers who used to shout 'take a look, buy a book' in the corridors of Connaught Place.

The book with the tempting sketches of the hedonist resting against a tree and drinking cups of heady wine from the hands of a sinuous saki under a full moon, sketches which, in a summer of artistic delusion, I had copied on chart paper and hung all over my room.

But the book was nowhere to be found; it had not survived the three dozen years and the dozen or so moves. Instead, I found three other *Rubaiyat* of Omar Khayyam; each an embodiment of pure physical beauty. The first, barely the size of a pocket dictionary, has a rich rust-brown cover depicting a medieval garden with intertwining branches, full-bodied roses, singing birds and fruits in the boughs. Each page featuring a single rubai, or quatrain in Persian, is framed like a carpet from the same land. The English version, with 102 rubais cramped into a few pages, is based on Edward Fitzgerald's translation from the first of his five editions. This edition can be distinguished from the later ones by slight differences in some of the rubais. The most famous of these is: Here with a loaf of bread beneath the bough,/A flask of wine, a book of verse and thou ...; in the third and later editions this becomes: A book of verses underneath the bough/A jug of wine, a loaf of bread—and thou ... I found this little gem of a book in the bookshop in the gardens of Hafiz's tomb in Shiraz, where newly-weds come to seek blessings and a turbaned dervish with deep-set eyes and a flowing beard walks around the chai-khanah.

The second is a very slim 1955 production that I found tucked away in a second-hand bookstore bursting at the seams. The rubais, again based on Fitzgerald's first edition, are all inscribed on dull yellow pages and the remarkable accompanying miniature depictions of hedonistic abandon are in the same yellow and pastel pink. This edition satisfies itself with seventy-five quatrains and ends with the emblematic signature phrase, Tamam Shud or: 'It is finished.'

And the third has nothing miniature about it; it is a large, lush and generous coffee-table book entitled *The Wine of Nishapur*, harking to the capital of Khorasan, which once rivalled Cairo and Baghdad and where Khayyam was born in 1048, as well as buried in 1131. This book is based on the belief that in order to fully understand Khayyam, it is not enough to master the Persian language; one has to be Iranian and have 'breathed the same air, felt the same spring breeze on his cheeks, enjoyed the same picnic in the meadow ...'

Using an all-Iranian team, it combines the English rendering of seventy-two rubais by Karim Emami and the skilful Persian calligraphy of Nasrollah Afje'i with the perceptive photography of the man who put it all together—Shahrokh Golestan. The photographs are a non-literal, philosophical take on Khayyam—red sunshades of a sidewalk café ('each Nowruz hold tulip-fashion a bowl of wine'), a long shadow of a passerby ('whence is the entrance

and whereto our exit?'), the sun's last rays on raindrops ('the moon will wax and wane over and over again') ...

Nobody quite knows how many rubais Khayyam actually wrote. In the oldest extant manuscript, copied 500 years ago in Shiraz and now held in the Bodleian Library, there are 158. In later versions, succeeding scribes added more until the total swelled to nearly 1200. Edward Fitzgerald culled out the essential ones and rendered them in a free English translation or, as he called it, a 'transmogrification', in 1859. He did not pretend to be too faithful to the original, often combining more than one rubai to make a brilliant whole that reads as one poem and not as separate epigrammatic quatrains. Incidentally, there was an Indian connection: his colleague, Prof. Edward Cowell discovered a Persian manuscript of the rubaiyat in the Asiatic Society of Calcutta and sent it to him. The resulting book went almost unnoticed and was soon in the one-penny boxes on the streets until it found admirers in the poets Rosetti and Swinburne (followed by Hardy, Eliot and Conan Doyle) and went on to become one of the most famous, essential and oft-quoted books for the next 100 years.

In his lifetime, Omar Khayyam was known not as a poet but as a philosopher, mathematician and astronomer. It is difficult to believe that his most influential work was a treatise that demonstrated the problems of algebra in which he solved cubic equations through intersecting conic sections; if you don't understand that, please join the club. He made far-reaching reforms to the Persian calendar, linking it to actual solar transit. He was in fact the precursor to non-Euclidian geometry and to a heliocentric view of the world. In addition, he wrote on mechanics, geography and jurisprudence.

It is for this work that the man—who has hundreds of wine-houses named after him—is also commemorated in a lunar crater on the far side of the moon and in a minor planet—3095 Omarkhayyam—discovered in 1980. One can only conclude that his scientific mind and philosophical bent questioned Divine providence and, finding no answers to the perplexities, he preferred to focus on the fleeting and sensual pleasures of the material world. Fitzgerald's rendering of Khayyam's rubaiyat has eclipsed the other achievements of this remarkable man, at least for the English-speaking world, in a manner best expressed by Khayyam himself:

Indeed the idols I have loved so long
Have done my credit in men's eye much wrong;
Have drowned my honour in a shallow cup
And sold my reputation for a song.

Poetry on a Perfect Pitch

The otherwise comfortable lounge at Istanbul airport had one major failing: its sockets did not match the plug on my laptop's charger. Even the duty-free shopping mall failed to produce the requisite number of pins in the desired shape. I shuddered at the prospect of spending the next eight hours twiddling my thumbs while all around me people cleared mail, chatted on Skype, swished tablet screens, smiled absently into cyberspace.

But the horror subsided as I discovered the saviour, suitably adorned in a cover the colour of green grass, in my hand baggage: *Cardus on Cricket*, a selection from the writings on the game by its most stylistic chronicler, Sir Neville Cardus. Turning away happily from the nightmare of the present—both my technological incapacity as well as the Indian team's tour of England—I slumped into a commodious leather chair and let myself be guided by a master into the sunlit past.

From his early background, it didn't seem that Cardus was born to write on cricket. Before he was fourteen he had earned money as a pavement artist, by pushing a builder's handcart, selling chocolates in a theatre and boiling printer's type. But the largely self-educated boy also discovered Dickens and an ambition to become a writer. He had also been bewitched by the style of A.C. Maclaren batting at Old Trafford; later he was to call the batsman 'the noblest Roman of them all'. Harbouring a passion for music, Cardus first became the dramatic critic for the *Manchester Guardian*. But in 1919 he fell ill and an inspired editor sent him away to relax and amuse himself by writing on cricket. He never stopped.

Cardus on Cricket contains excerpts from books that appeared from 1922 to 1937 so the descriptions are mostly of English and Australian (he spent seven years Down Under) cricketers, with the sole exception of the West Indian, Constantine. For Cardus, cricket is quintessentially an English game: 'Where the English language is unspoken there can be no real cricket ... In every English village a cricket field is as much part of the landscape as the old church.' His cricket is also a summer game, its season starting with the freshness of spring in April and dying with the melancholic approach of autumn. It is in the English setting, be it a Test match at Lord's or a Saturday match on a village green that Cardus is at his most poetic, gently infusing romance, nostalgia and yearning into the game as he describes 'cricket to the sound of somebody clipping a hedge on a June morning; cricket to the sound of a bird singing or of a dog barking a long way distant ...' One cannot help thinking that an Indian Cardus, were he to emerge, would similarly find poetry in cricket being played in the winter sun, when the sound of willow on leather ball hides the cracking of peanut shells underfoot, and the tanginess of oranges being peeled fills the stands. And he may find enough Indian-English creativity, including shouts of Howzat, amidst the dozens of games simultaneously happening in streets and lanes, with stumps sketched on walls with charcoal or hastily put up with stolen bricks, from Dadar to Dehra Dun.

Cardus writes with as much poetic passion of cricket's dramatic moments as he does of the men who made the game. He tells of the bearded Master—W.G. Grace—who was asked how he could stop the shooting ball infallibly in the days of fast, slinging bowling on very rough pitches. And he answered, Mallory-like, 'Why, you put your bat to the ball.' Or of the Australian fast bowler Macdonald, 'a Lucifer of his craft ... running along a curve silently, his arm sinuous, his wrist poising the ball before letting it go— the cobra's poise.' He describes thus the flight of the spinner Wilfred Rhodes: 'the curving line, now higher, now lower, tempting, inimical, every ball like every other ball, yet somehow unlike; every ball a decoy, a spy sent out to get the lie of the land; some balls simple, some complex, some easy, some difficult; and one of them—ah, which?—the master ball.' There is the artist-batsman Hammond who 'provides criticism with a criterion, a standard' and Jack Hobbs, whose style 'like the style of the master in every art, and of every fine art, seems to sum up all that has gone before in the development of his technique.' Cardus quite

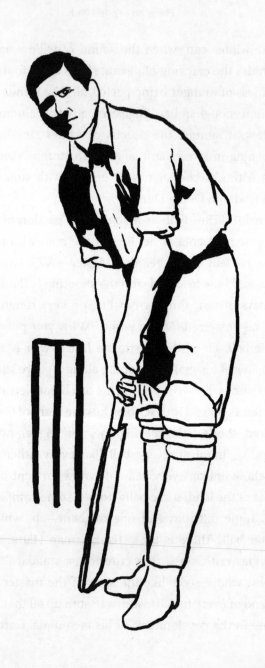

loses all restraint when he comes to Frank Woolley, whose 'cricket is compounded of soft airs and fresh flavours. The bloom of the year is on it, making for sweetness. And the very brevity of summer is in it too, making for loveliness ... he is always about to lose his wicket; his runs are thin-spun. His bat is charmed and most of us, being reasonable, do not believe in charms. There is a miracle happening on every cricket field when Woolley stays in two or three hours; an innings by him is almost too unsubstantial for this world ...' And he yearns for a mis-hit or a duck from Bradman to bring back the glorious uncertainties of cricket.

What of Indian greats, you may well ask. The selection contains two references. One, of course, is to Ranjitsinhji, whom Cardus described as 'entirely original ... his style was a remarkable instance of the way a man can express personal genius in a game—nay, not only a personal genius but the genius of a whole race ... When he batted a strange light was seen for the first time on English fields, a light out of the East.' Ranji defied all the Victorian straightforwardness of English cricket, symbolized by the straight bat and good-length ball; his presence was a 'dusky, supple legerdemain' in a rippling silk shirt that charmed away good-length balls to the fine leg boundary with a flick of the wrist. 'Bowlers stood transfixed,' writes Cardus, 'and possibly crossed themselves.' The second reference is to the Nawab of Pataudi senior, who was part of the leg trap set by Jardine for Larwood during the Bodyline tour of Australia. When Larwood unleashed his thunderbolts to Bradman,

Jardine ordered the Nawab to move closer and closer to the Don's left pocket until 'Pataudi sits under Bradman's chin, and notices how carefully he has shaved today'. One wonders what Cardus would have done with a Gavaskar or a Tendulkar as raw material but somehow I feel he would have revelled in the romance of Tiger Pataudi—the Nawabi touch, the Sussex chapter, the rising to sudden captaincy at twenty-one as Contractor is felled by Charlie Griffith, the uncertainties and unspoken possibilities caused by the car accident—would have all been grist to the poetic mill.

But perhaps it is just as well that Cardus stopped writing when he did. If he had lived on, he may not have felt at home in the Technicolor world of cricket after Kerry Packer. T-20 would have shocked him, IPL would have made him nauseous and the mention of a third umpire or hot-spot would surely have made him turn back to dramatic criticism.

Thank God for the sockets in that lounge. Sometimes, to see the stars, we need the lights to go out.

The Chatterley Hat Trick

Not the most felicitous of metaphors to use when India has crashed to a humiliating defeat at Trent Bridge but in book-hunting, like in cricket, one can sometimes bag a hat trick. And so it was when I found, on the dollar shelf outside a second-hand bookshop, three books placed in a manner that would bring an approving smile to the face of the most fastidious librarian. An unexpurgated edition of *Lady Chatterley's Lover* was neatly sandwiched between *The First Lady Chatterley* and *The Trial of Lady Chatterley*. To pick them all up was a matter of moments; to read and discuss all three can take much longer.

But briefly, *Lady Chatterley's Lover*, read more than eight decades after it was written, is hardly likely to shock. Constance, or Connie, is married to Clifford, a minor baron in a fast industrialising England. The marriage is unhappy, incomplete and distant, not the least because Clifford has been left paralysed below the waist by the War. Struggling with her sexual frustration and loneliness, Connie finds happiness, love and a child in the arms of Clifford's gamekeeper, Mellors. There are elaborate descriptions of the physical union, sympathy for the adulterous relationship, beautiful and sensual writing, some ridiculous passages and a generous sprinkling of well-known Anglo-Saxon four-letter words, not usually found in such novels. There is also some half-hearted polemic against a sick, industrialized society prostrating itself at the feet of the 'bitch Goddess of Success' set against the ideal world of nature and the soul in which human relationships are based on mutual respect, or reverence, as Lawrence would have it. And there is the connection with India, where Mellors has served as an army officer. The rest is the baggage of this book's dramatic publishing history that has made it synonymous with teenage titillation, steamy writing, and the banning of books. But for this baggage, the book may not have attracted half the fame—or notoriety—that it did.

The second book, *The First Lady Chatterley*, was the first of the three drafts of the book that Lawrence wrote, between 1925 and 1928, in a pinewood in the Tuscan hills. He wrote sitting absolutely still on a stone slab in a cave with another stone slab as a table with a spring gurgling close by, not far from olive trees, mint and thyme, wild gladioli, violets and myrtle shrubs. This first draft was published in 1944 with a loving foreword by his wife Frieda, who regarded it as her favourite of the three versions. The story is the same but modern literature's most famous gamekeeper Mellors is known here as Parkin and the 'purple passages' that were to so shock the keepers of the world's conscience are missing. The first version was too gentle, too mystic, too tender for a Lawrence wishing to revolt against the bounds of a genteel society and the demands of censor-morons, as he called them. He wanted to add punch and so he produced his 'taboo-shattering bomb'.

But it is *The Trial of Lady Chatterley* that is the most engrossing. It is a sharply edited transcript of the case of Regina v. Penguin Books Limited, fought at the Old Bailey in October 1960. Penguin had advertised an unexpurgated publication of the book and obviously expecting quick sales had printed 200,000 copies. The Director of Public Prosecution, obtaining a copy from the notorious booksellers of Charing Cross, challenged the publication under the Obscene Publications Act of 1959, which

ironically had been brought in to prevent pornography but protect literature. Penguin then sent across twelve copies for the jurors, ordinary men and women, who read them comfortably ensconced in deep leather armchairs. The test was simple: the jurors were to decide if the book, read as a whole, was such that would 'tend to deprave or corrupt persons' who were likely to read it; and if so, was there sufficient public good in the interest of science, literature, art etc., to still justify its publication?

Brilliant arguments were advanced from both sides. The prosecution argued that the book put adultery and promiscuity on a pedestal, that the narrative described only a series of sexual encounters and the polemic against industrialisation was mere padding. There was unnecessary use of coarse language (there is something inherently amusing in a proper barrister at the Old Bailey toting up the number of times each of the famous four-letter words has been used) and, available widely for three and a half shillings, the book would 'tend to deprave and corrupt' without any countering literary merit. The defence was elaborately organized and brought forward thirty-five witnesses—men and women of letters, including E.M. Forster, teachers, moral theologians—to expound on the literary merits of the book. Lawrence was portrayed as Britain's greatest novelist since Hardy. One witness called the book 'virtuous and puritanical'; another called it an argument in favour of marriage—but not just a legal marriage (!)—since Connie and Mellors want to marry;

another an allegory in which all the sex is simply a 'return to the soul' in a mechanized, sick world. Lawrence had wanted to show the importance of human relationships and, most importantly, the man–woman relationship in its physical and emotional wholeness. As to his use of four-letter words, he wanted to drag them out of their shameful connotations and thus purify them; only then could sex, which he called 'valid and precious', be spoken about as something pure and normal. After six days of hearings, the jury took only three hours to reach the unanimous verdict of 'Not Guilty'. It was never clarified whether that meant 'not obscene' or 'obscene but justified'. The judge refused to pass an order regarding costs, which at £13,000 probably made this the most expensive seminar on Lawrence's writing. Penguin was allowed to publish the unexpurgated version in the UK, thirty-two years after the author's death, and they chose to dedicate the publication to the twelve jurors who made it possible.

Four years later, a five-member bench of the Supreme Court of India in the case of *Ranjit Udeshi* v. *State of Maharashtra* held that the book met the test for obscenity and there was no social good arising out of it that would justify its publication in India. Justice Hidyatullah's judgment, whether one agrees with it or not, is worth reading for its coruscating brilliance and analysis of Lawrence's personality.

Fondling the Details

The literary café is the most exciting part of the biennial Jerusalem Book Fair. In this open, informal and civilized space—in fact, so civilized that it has a working coffee counter right next to a makeshift stage—take place the encounters with the literary giants of home and abroad. I was witness to one such interaction a few years ago: The man on the spot was Britain's foremost writer: Ian McEwan, winner of the Jerusalem Prize, and the man who expertly drew him out, with an understated knowledge of literary technique and rapier sharp wit, was Meir Shelev, himself a renowned Israeli novelist.

McEwan's response on being given the Jerusalem Prize was suitably self-deprecatory, as if constantly looking back over his shoulder to make sure that the judges had not made some mistake. He paid homage to other recipients before him, people who had 'rearranged his mind'. The list that begins with the philosopher Bertrand Russell includes Simone de Beauvoir, who provided special insights into relationships; Isaiah Berlin, who had shown the 'dangers of Utopia', as well as fiction writers Arthur Miller and Milan Kundera, whose fiction 'swayed and entranced him'.

From the prize itself to the city after which it is named was a natural jump. Shelev trawled out the not-so-complimentary reactions to Jerusalem of some famous writers. Herman Melville, on visiting Jerusalem, said that 'Jerusalem is surrounded by cemeteries and dead people are its strongest guild.' Actually, though Shelev did not venture that far, Melville said much more and his descriptions would never make it to a tourist brochure. He thought that Jerusalem looks at you 'like a cold, gray eye in a cold, old man ... Stony mountains & stony plains; stony walls & stony fields; stony houses & stony tombs; stony eyes & stony hearts. Before you and behind you are stones.' Gogol was so affected by the city that on his return he burnt the second half of *Dead Souls*. McEwan agrees that the city has a 'sense of echo' and could well destroy his novel in progress. Like a sudden journey, which can startle you with a new insight into life and make everything written earlier sound meaningless and trite.

However, the city's preoccupation with religion does not get to him. Ever the outspoken rationalist, he proclaims his atheism and the absence of any divine force dictating the affairs of men. 'Most things that happen in life are random. You may not have been born if, say on one evening in 1948, your mother had decided to stay in and wash her hair instead of going out to a party where she met this nice young man.' Much in the same manner, he proclaims, the novel is constructed of a series of coincidences that enable the interaction between characters and move the action forward. When the conversation turns, as inevitably such conversations turn nowadays, to the issue of the survival of the novel, McEwan offers an irresistible rationale for its survival: 'Human beings are social animals, profoundly curious about each other's lives. The novel is a kind of higher form of gossip and is sustained by our curiosity about others. It satisfies our gossipy instincts. Jane Austen was the greatest and most gossipy of novelists.'

But it is of the novella, a form with which he has had 'an enduring love affair,' that he talks enthusiastically. It is this genre that he enjoys most; even *On Chesil Beach* is only 39,000 words long; it enables the writer to move the story ahead at a tremendous speed, leaving no place for subplots. In a way he is a miniaturist: a confined place—whether in space or time—seems to bring out the best in him, the little visual detail, the description of every half-movement, the cranking up of the literary tension, bit by bit.

As he admits elsewhere, he has always kept in mind Nabokov's directive to 'fondle details.' So he plays around with sentences, replaces one word with another, polishes passages until it seems that they were always meant to be as they finally appear. The process is as much for the pleasure of the writer as it is for the reader; in fact, it is a 'self-pleasuring act'. His literary career began with two collections of short stories and whimsically he muses that that is where it may well end: 'Writing a novel needs stamina. I find it exhausting to be in the foothills of a novel. In my eighties, I see myself folding completely into the novella, then into the short story, then perhaps into haiku.'

On the mechanics of writing, the tiring 'procedural questions': he likes to think of every novel as his first. The exhausting post-book activity, when the author has to peddle his book in the manner of a salesman of glass tiles, deadens the book in the author's mind. He is then free to move on. That's McEwan's preference too.

He likes gaps between books, he 'tries to let some life go by'. As he said in an interview some time ago: 'I'm very cautious about starting anything without letting time go, and feeling it's got to come out. I'm quite good at not writing. Some people are tied to five hundred words a day, six days a week. I'm a hesitater.' When he does start writing, it is a tentative process—putting down fragments, introducing characters to see what they would do. He is elated by surprises, the surprise of a particular adjective appearing before a noun or a character making a sudden move; 'in fact', he says, 'a character should surprise you.' As one would expect, McEwan writes down ideas, images and phrases as they come in a spiral notebook. He relates how once, when writing notes in a café, he lost his notebook, leaving him with a feeling of tremendous loss. Until one day, eighteen months later, the notebook landed, in a brown envelope, with a thud on his doormat. On re-reading it, he discovered that it did not contain a single worthy thought!

As I left the café, I bought not one of his famous novels but a collection of early short stories, *In Between the Sheets*. I'm only halfway through it, and I certainly don't want to hurry him along to his eighties, but so powerful is his short stuff that I look forward to the time when Ian McEwan will 'fold into the novella'.

Immortality in a Test-tube

Often it is the sheer creative power of literary fiction, or the beauty of chiselled prose or the lyricism of poetic writing that propels one to write about a book. On some occasions, as in the case of *The Immortal Life of Henrietta Lacks* by Rebecca Skloot, it is the raw power of a true story and the commitment of a non-fiction writer to unearth that story that can leave the reader drawing in one sharp breath after another. This brave, scary, raw book in which 'no names have been changed, no characters invented, no events fabricated' tells a strange story based on a potent mix of scientific discoveries, deadly disease, racial discrimination, medical ethics, love and devotion.

First, the bare facts: In October 1951, an African-American woman called Henrietta Lacks, descendant of slaves and a poor Southern tobacco farmer herself, died of a vicious case of cervical cancer at the Johns Hopkins hospital in Baltimore. Days before her death, and without her knowledge or consent, doctors took a slice of her tumour and passed it on to the laboratory of Dr George Gey, who had been trying unsuccessfully to grow human cells. Henrietta's cells not only grew in Gey's test tubes but they multiplied at a terrifying rate. These cells, known as HeLa, after her initials, were not only packaged, gifted, sold and shipped across the world but also sent into space. Soon they became the standard workhorse of research labs the world over. If all the HeLa cells that have been produced were weighed, they would add up to 50 million metric tonnes and if laid out, they would wrap around the earth three times.

HeLa cells were used for studying cancer, gene-mapping, cloning, chemotherapy, in-vitro fertilization and several other areas of medical research; they were critical in the development of the polio vaccine. The sad part of the story is that for twenty years Henrietta's husband and children did not know that an entire medical industry had built up around her cells while they themselves could often not afford medical insurance. And the world did not know her correct name (sometimes the pseudonym Helen Lane appeared), or that she was black. It would take a further thirty years—until the publication of this book—for the entire story to come out. As for Henrietta, she was buried in an unmarked grave not far from the log cabin in Clover, Virginia, where she had been raised.

Along comes Rebecca Skloot, a biology student turned science writer, who becomes obsessed with the desire to find out all there is about Henrietta Lacks and to tell her story.

And so begins a decade-long adventure during which she patiently and with tremendous empathy uncovers the details of Henrietta's impoverished past, her short and brave battle with her incurable disease, the miseries that befell her children.

The story emerges bit by bit, after hundreds of hours of interviews with Henrietta's close and distant family members, neighbours, cousins, doctors, scientists, other writers. En route we get rich, varied and disturbing glimpses into different aspects of American life of the early and middle twentieth century.

Of beat-up, desolate strip towns in the middle of nowhere, of uneducated African-American children working from dawn to dusk in tobacco farms, of workers facing asbestos exposure, of the days when it was still acceptable to call people 'coloured' and have 'coloured'

wards, examination rooms, drinking fountains, of a time when there was a Hospital of the Negro Insane.

We also visit with Skloot the murky world of scientific research, of the Tuskegee syphilis study where hundreds of African-American men were allowed to die slow, painful and preventable deaths and of Mississippi Appendectomies, where unnecessary hysterectomies were performed on poor African-American women, all in the name of research. And of an American doctor called Chester Southam who injected cancerous cells into hundreds of patients without their consent to prove a scientific point, only a few years after the Nuremberg trials where seven Nazi doctors had been sentenced to death by hanging for similar 'research' without consent.

The emotional core of the book is the relationship that Skloot manages to establish with Henrietta's children, particularly with her resilient and character-laden daughter Deborah. For this she has to fight through their deep-seated fear about further exploitation, their sense of injustice about not being told what really happened to their mother, their poverty as against the advances made through use of her cells, their struggle to accept that in some ways their mother truly has become immortal.

Their search, as we see, is not only for material compensation but for emotional closure. As Deborah says: *'People got rich off my mother without us knowin about them takin her cells, now we don't get a dime. I used to go so mad about that to where it made me sick and I had to take pills. But I don't got it in me no more to fight. I just want to know who my mother was ... I want to know, what did my mother smell like? For all my life I just don't know anything, not even the little common things, like what color she like? Did she like to dance? Did she breastfeed me? Lord, I'd like to know that. But nobody ever say nothing.'*

Closure comes, when Skloot manages to take Deborah and her brother into Hopkins and show them their mother's cells through a microscope, still living and dividing under their very eyes.

And further closure came in February 2011 when the State Legislature of Virginia resolved to 'celebrate the life of Henrietta Lacks, in honor of all who have ever faced discrimination and exploitation, and her amazing legacy, which has altered medical research and care and relieved the suffering of untold millions'. This too would not have happened if not for this courageous book.

Fact, Fiction and the Travel Urge

Dreams are still not taxable so here's one more: having bumped around the world enough, and not much in India, I take a deep red jeep, all fitted out and well-stocked, and drive for six months, all the way up from the brittle emptiness of Ladakh through the crowded heartland, down the Konkan coast and up the Coromandel, across the little-explored North-east, through snow, heat, dust and monsoon downpour. Eating roadside, sleeping under the stars, talking to strangers, keeping furious notes. And for company, the highly intelligent best friend, Dara, my German shepherd. That's not an original idea of course; it's been done before. In 1960, an ailing, fifty-eight-year-old John Steinbeck, waning as a novelist, set out for an eleven-week trip across America in an outfitted pick-up truck with his French poodle Charley. The result was the highly acclaimed classic of American travel writing, *Travels with Charley*.

Steinbeck confesses to an incurable travel urge. 'The sound of a jet, an engine warming up, even the clopping of shod hooves on pavement brings on the ancient shudder, the dry mouth and vacant eye, the hot palms and the churn of stomach high up under the rib cage ... once a bum always a bum.' And so he let himself ease off into the great American night in a rough counter-clockwise loop that takes him and Charley up to Maine, then across the northern states to the Pacific coast, down to California and then back along the southern route. The book does not record an exact diary; instead, it depicts the writer's thoughts and musings as he drives, interwoven with local descriptions of landscape, speech and people. Every once in a while there is an interaction with a stranger—a farmer in north Michigan, a Shakespearean actor in the middle of nowhere in North Dakota, a virulent racist in Louisiana. Interspersed among the conversations and descriptions are the writer's extended views on subjects as diverse as racial segregation, the giant Californian redwoods and all things Texan. ('Texas is a state of mind. Texas is an obsession.') There are places, says Steinbeck, 'where fable, myth, preconception, love, longing, or prejudice step in and so distort a cool, clear appraisal that a kind of high-colored magical confusion takes permanent hold. Greece is such an area, and those parts of England where King Arthur walked ... And surely Texas is such a place.'

Charley and his antics, his French-gentleman breeding which makes him believe that 'humans are nuts', his prostatitis and his hilarious encounter with a vet nursing a hangover get ample play in the journey and it's touching to see Steinbeck conducting conversations with the dog on matters such as the search for roots. ('He listened but he didn't reply.') Charley fortunately 'doesn't belong to a species clever enough to split the atom but not clever enough to live in peace with itself'.

Particularly enchanting is the wisdom about travel and travel writing that is strewn casually about. Each journey, Steinbeck believes, is like a person; with an individuality and temperament that is impossible to control and bind down with schedules and reservations. 'We do not take a trip,' he says, 'a trip takes us.' Many trips continue in the mind long after movement in space and time has ceased; others leave us 'without warning, or good-bye or kiss my foot' while we are still stranded far from home. Steinbeck's trip ended for him while he was still in Virginia; from then on the 'road became a stone ribbon, the hills obstructions, the trees green blurs, the people simply moving figures with heads but no faces'. Steinbeck confesses he kept few notes

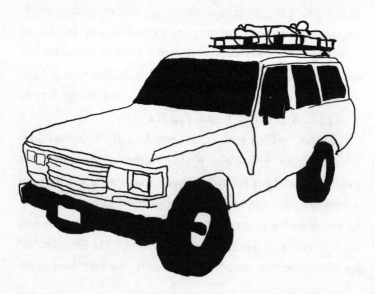

about his journey and is surprised to find some scribblings bound to a ketchup bottle with a rubber band. The large macrocosm of the land is the macrocosm of himself; to anybody else it would be different. External reality is not so external; it depends on whose eye surveys it. Each person brings home a different city, a different journey, a different truth. 'So much there is to see, but our morning eyes describe a different world than do our afternoon eyes, and surely our wearied evening eyes can report only a weary evening world.'

And now, a full fifty-odd years later, along comes a journalist named Bill Steigerwald to spoil the party. A Steinbeck fan, he set out to commemorate the journey by following the Nobel laureate's wheel tracks and write a book on how America has changed. Instead, he ended up finding drastic discrepancies in Steinbeck's account. Using biographies of Steinbeck, letters that he wrote from the road, newspaper articles and the first draft of the book, he contends that Steinbeck was not predominantly alone during the journey but was joined by his wife, that he did not sleep in the camper under the stars too often but in motels and even luxury hotels and that several of the encounters he writes about, including the charming one with the thespian, actually never happened. And now readers and scholars are divided between those who feel let down by their literary hero for palming off fiction as non-fiction and those who say that it really doesn't matter that much; after all, all non-fiction contains some fiction (remember Chatwin?) and the book does remain a quirky, entertaining classic. As Steigerwald himself writes: 'It doesn't matter if it's not the true or full or honest story of Steinbeck's quixotic road trip. It was never meant to be. It's a metaphor, a work of art, not a AAA travelogue. Steinbeck himself insisted in "Charley"—a little defensively—that he wasn't trying to write a travelogue or do real journalism. And he points out more than once that his trip was subjective and uniquely his, and so was its retelling.'

And I'll keep that in mind when I recount what Dara and I talked about. No slight to poodles, but a German shepherd might even reply.

The Lone Ranger of the Steppes

Captain Frederick Burnaby of the Blues regiment of the British Army was quite a man. Six feet four inches tall and with a chest that measured 47 inches, he could carry a small pony under one arm. Yet he was agile enough to be able to vault across the regimental billiards table and brainy enough to be fluent in French, Italian, German, Russian and Spanish, not to mention a working knowledge of Turkish and Arabic. He was a relentless adventurer, even crossing the English Channel solo in a balloon at ten thousand feet, and when he took a break from all this, his distinctive prose style ensured that he was employed by *The Times* and other Fleet Street journals to cover foreign campaigns.

It was the time of the Great Game, the tussle for strategic advantage being played out on the wind-swept steppes of Central Asia between the British and the Russians. It was a time of feint and counter-feint, courageous espionage and devilish diplomacy in the most exotic of settings with names as evocative as Bokhara and Samarkand ... And the prize was the fabled land beyond the Himalayas: Hindostan. The Russians were moving fast across Central Asia, swallowing up khanate after khanate and only the

Turcoman territories separated them from Kabul and the Khyber Pass. If they were to ever really threaten British India, they would need important staging points, including the towns of Merv, Khiva, Balkh and Kashgar. Russian analysts were convinced that native India would rise to welcome them, the East India company being 'a poisonous unnatural plant engrafted on the splendid soil of India—a parasite which saps away the life of the most fertile and wealthy country in the world'. British opinion was divided: men like Burnaby believed that Russian advances had to be challenged and to be seen for what they were while others preferred the thought of a Russian neighbour in contrast to the 'barbarous Afghans', or believed that the threat was not real: India would last their lifetime anyway.

It was in this political context that the burly Burnaby, resting in Khartoum after a journey to the White Nile, came across a news snippet that hit him like a challenging glove across the face: The St Petersburg government had decreed that foreigners were not to be allowed to travel in Russian Asia. He determined immediately to re-attempt a journey that typhoid had forced him to give up earlier; all the way to Khiva, east of the Aral Sea, fabled caravan city, an infamous slave market and now only nominally autonomous; the Russians were within

striking distance. And never mind that it was winter; that was when he had his furlough and he could not wait for fair weather.

Burnaby's incredible journey from London's Victoria Station to the Khivan bazaar is recorded in the first of his two Great Game classics, *A Ride to Khiva*. Both this book and sequel *On Horseback through Asia Minor*, were bestsellers and the basis of entire library shelves of Great Game literature, including the tremendously gripping work of Peter Hopkirk. He makes it by train to St Petersburg in three and a half days, armed with a sail cloth sleeping tent which he would be unable to get into, the thickest Scottish fishing stockings, fur-lined shoes, jerseys and flannels galore, a regulation revolver with twenty cartridges, thermometer, barometer, sextant, cutlery and of course quinine, without which an Englishman wouldn't set out until they invented the more agreeable gin and Indian tonic water.

Thence, it becomes a typically Russian journey, full of charm and bureaucracy, bribery and generosity, across two thousand miles by train, sleigh—both horse and camel driven—and finally horseback into the inhospitable wild. On the way Burnaby overcomes huge challenges— unrelenting weather, cold that defines cold, debilitating frostbite—but retains the objectivity to relate the story of his journey with political insight, literary turn of phrase and, above all, an irrepressible sense of humour. Burnaby is hard on the Russians on the road, especially their personal hygiene habits. Again and again there comes upon him a yearning for soap and water: 'If the Russian peasant could be persuaded to be more particular in his ablutions, it would be conducive, if not to his own comfort at least to that of his fellow-travellers.' His comfort whenever he can manage to have a bath is palpable. He also remarks frequently on the rather unusual culinary predilections of his companions on the road. He partakes of a mixture of rice, eggs and chocolate boiled in milk, cuts frozen bread with an axe as a mere knife would break and watches his companions eating half-cooked horseflesh and rice straight out of the cauldron. The bottom line is that a hungry man, ravaged by that fierce cold, can eat and enjoy almost anything: '... after a ride across the steppes in midwinter the traveller soon loses every other feeling than the absorbing one of hunger, and at that time I think I could have eaten my great grandfather if he had been properly roasted for the occasion.'

Burnaby also makes the charming discovery that Kirghiz poetry is full of odes in honour of sheep, an animal that is 'placed on the highest pinnacle of their estimation; after their wives and, indeed, sometimes before them.' A 100 sheep is the average price for a bride, whom the Kirghiz has the advantage of seeing unveiled unlike the less nomadic of the Tartars. The ideal of beauty, an ideal that is constantly beyond Burnaby's understanding, is a moon-faced girl with sheep's eyes! In fact, at one stage, bewitched by the beauty of a young Kirghiz widow, Burnaby begins to pay her compliments in Russian and is dismayed to learn that his interpreter translated them into Tartar as: 'thou are lovelier than a sheep with a fat tail'—this appendage being regarded a great delicacy—and 'thy face is the roundest in the flock, and that thy breath is sweeter than many pieces of mutton roasted over bright embers'.

Burnaby did reach Khiva by clever design and dodge and entered a town of 'richly painted minarets and high domes of coloured tiles'. Contrary to all the legends he had heard about the cruelties of the Asiatic Khan, he was received by a courteous and hospitable ruler with a genial smile and a twinkle in his eye and a burning curiosity about geography and politics. To some disappointment, Burnaby had to answer in the negative when asked whether the British queen could order the chopping off of her subject's head or the slitting of his throat. But, for me, the book ended when the Khan said 'Hindostan is a very wonderful country' and proceeded to gift Burnaby a long robe lined with silk and brightly coloured chintzes. Burnaby insisted on calling this a dressing gown though it was the equivalent then of getting the Order of the Garter in England.

Grace of the Unspoken

Floating thoughts, an intercepted glance, a snatch of conversation overheard, a book picked at random from an apple box outside a second-hand bookshop: in such things, given the right moment, often lie the seeds of an essay, a poem, a short story and—for the fortunate few—a novel. And so it seems is the case for this column.

A yellowing news cutting in my files about the lost art of written correspondence, a few old Hindi songs at dusk and a news item mourning the closure, in a small border town, of the municipal library with a picture of the crestfallen faces of helpless children and elderly citizens. Alone, each of these is just a stray event, at best a sentimental paean for a vanished past or a grudging salute to the juggernaut of technology. Taken together, especially on a windy night when a lone lit-up boat is the only thing that breaks the inky darkness of the sea and sky, these things fall into the finality of a pattern, reminding us of all that has slipped unknowing through our fingers while we were looking elsewhere, signalling a loss that has already become irretrievable even as we become aware of it.

The news cutting is just a book review, but the book

is enticingly called *Yours Ever*. Written over several years by Thomas Mallon, during which our hesitant handshake with e-mails over screeching modems has turned into a twenty-four-hour addictive embrace, it is an elegy to the art of letter writing. Among those whose letters make up the meat of the book are several writers, including Flaubert, William Faulkner, F. Scott Fitzgerald and Ralph Waldo Emerson. Nothing reveals better the mind of a writer, or for that matter, of a president or a king or a lover, than a letter written by him. Separated by decades or by centuries, the reader can feel the writer's torture congealed in the long dried ink, the passion in the folds of carefully chosen paper, the hesitation in the little postscript, the doubt in the scratched-out sentence ... Seen in this manner, these letters become the lifeblood of historical research, the insight that brings biography alive.

When writing my own novel, *The Exile*, I searched for, and found, Maharaja Duleep Singh's voice in a handful of his letters that I read one stolen afternoon in the British Library. His handwriting, his phrasing, his choice of words—all became windows into his mind and then his soul. I wonder what the biographers or writers of historical fiction will do when they have to reopen the secrets of our digital age. What will replace these letters? Where will they find the cache of personal e-mails, the confessions, the fears, the advice, the justification, the evasion that will give the third dimension to their subjects? Which spouse, or child, or one-time sweetheart will keep these e-mails tied up in a ribbon or carefully folded into an old tin candy box?

The loss is greater than simply the difficulties that will be faced by the researchers of the future; no doubt they will invent some virtual bank where it will all be archived. Perhaps some imaginative minds and sensitive souls will reinvent the postal system as a speedy and safe courier service and even find ways to retain the old colonial buildings that were our best post offices, turning them into philatelic museums and internet cafés.

But how will one ever explain to the next generation the anticipation that rose to fever pitch as one waited for the tinkle of the bicycle bell of the khaki-clad, peak-capped postman in the hot summer afternoons. Or the disappointment that his consoling smile never quite wiped out on the days that brought no letter. Or the smell of sealing wax when sending a birthday parcel, or the glue-laden brushes that covered not only the back of the stamp but also the thumb and forefinger, or the rush for putting a letter at the last minute into a stunted, red pillar box marked 'late fee delivery' or the sight of the huge bags being thrown into red vans in the gathering dusk behind the post office as if they were being sent into nowhere, or the pleasure of walking a mile on fallen pine needles to the little hill post office and finding a letter with your name waiting there labelled 'Poste Restante'. Something has vanished in this trade-off for instant communication, some romance, some mystery.

Or quite simply, some grace.

Perhaps it is the same vanished grace that haunts the old songs that burnished the edges of the twilight today; it's breathing in the lilt of those melodies or the obliqueness of the lyrics. The same wordless quality that could suffuse Waheeda Rahman's eyes with loss and regret in a haunting shot in a deserted film studio, lit only by a strobe of sunlight from an open skylight. Or that enabled Meena Kumari to convey passion, intoxication, taunt and promise in one look as she fought to keep her zamindar husband away from the dancing girls. Or that lay, like his rough coat, on Guru Dutt's hunched shoulders, with all the heaviness of defeat and frustration. Nothing much needed to be said after that, the unspoken said it all. It is not mere sentimentalism or nostalgia when one fails to find this grace of the unsaid, the romance of the unspoken, the passion that smoulders, in a world in which Shah Rukh Khan acts as Shah Rukh Khan in movie after movie, where Salman Khan's shirt magically unbuttons itself and falls off to reveal the rippling stuff and Munni competes in a torso-twisting tussle with Sheila.

The battle is already lost, but there are consolations in minor acts of rebellion. The use of a fountain pen, a soft creamy paper diary, an occasional note written on an inland letter and posted to an unsuspecting friend from a remote post office, a walk through the shelves of an old library, inhaling the smell of old books and talcum powder ... Perhaps all these put together will form another pattern: an old-fashioned salaam to times that were.

Twitterature: What Next?

The Great Gatsby, often voted the last century's best novel, reduced to 16 twitter posts, each well within the 140 character limit, counting spaces ... No, I'm not making this up on the strength of too much Christmas rum cake and nor is it some New Year gag. It has actually happened and that too in a very respectable, pure orange and classy cream Penguin book called *Twitterature*. And not to the Gatsby alone but to many other greats too ... Shakespeare, Homer, Kafka, Hemingway, Woolf, Pushkin ... you name them.

So what does it sound like? Let's go back to Gatsby, holding my broken heart. In the fourth tweet, Nick, the elegant, understated, sensitive narrator has this to say: 'Some dude is standing on the bay with his arms up looking at a symbolic light. The Midwest didn't have so many metaphors! What a CREEP!' And somewhere towards the book's poignant end, he continues: 'Gatsby is so emo. Who cries about his girlfriend while eating breakfast ... IN THE POOL?'

Or turn to Shakespeare's Macbeth, whose fabulous resounding soliloquies we committed to memory in school and listen to how he describes his own end: 'Shit.

"C-Section" is not "of woman born"? What kind of King dies on a goddamn technicality?' And here is Hamlet for you: 'Gonna try to talk some sense into Mom because boyfriend completely killed Dad. I sense this is the moment of truth, the moment of candour and—'

Old King Lear is not to be left out of this mass murder of the great tragedies. He ruminates: 'What, my ungrateful girls are kicking me out? I'll be cold and homeless. This sucketh. Very unexpected. Am I right?'

The Russian greats, who captured the tragic nuances of the Russian soul in their tomes, do not escape the onslaught of this great invention of social media. Gogol, in his *Overcoat*, exclaims, 'OMG my coat is gone. Everything is ruined. </3' (For the innocent, that mathematical-looking icon is meant to signify annoyance, a broken heart, super irony in twitter lingo.) And ends the famous tale with the tweet: 'I suppose I have what I want now, it's time to rest. If anyone sees my coat, tweet it.' *Anna Karenina* ends, after her suicide, with the words: 'This user's account has been deactivated.' The classic duel scene in Pushkin's *Eugene Onegin* can be summarized as: 'Wanna hear something really funny? I try to sleep with his wife, he challenges me to a duel, I shoot him and he dies!' The central crime in Dostoevsky's *Crime and Punishment* is tweeted thus: 'Casually off'd that old maid while typing this. Some other bitch walked in ... well, she's dead too. Bad timing, LOL.

If this was all meant to be funny, it would be, well, funny. But the scary thing is that this is for real, an exercise in pure earnest. The authors anticipate that their effort would be criticized as a travesty of great works so they justify it in a laboured introduction. They believe that the classics of literature are inaccessible and outdated in their original form and set out to remedy this much in the manner, according to their own opinion, as a Martin Luther undertaking the Reformation and popularising the Scripture. By reducing these classics to tweets, they hope to bring not their 'dull, dull words' but their 'raw insight into humanity' to the reading public in an 'instant-publishing, short-attention-span, all-digital-all-the-time, self-important age of info-deluge.' They seriously believe that they 'have liberated poor Hamlet from the rigorous literary constraints of the sixteenth century and made him—without losing an ounce of wisdom, beauty, wit or angst—a happening youngster.'

It is this seriousness of intent that makes the entire thing so dangerous. My mind goes back to the 1960s and sees a young boy cycling purposefully to a small shop in a lane off Dehradun's Paltan bazaar. There a smiling old man in a loose kurta-pyjama would sell him Classics Illustrated at twenty-five paise apiece. The boy would bind them and treasure them and hungrily devour them in curtained rooms during the long summer afternoons. *Wuthering Heights, Julius Caeser, Jane Eyre ...*

Even if he went on to read some of them in their full, original, daunting form, it was their illustrated versions he would remember. By the same token, I fear that forty years on some reader may only recall the classics through the tweets. Forever he may remember Frankenstein as 'This killing thing is getting way out of control. You know like a mistress you can't shut up?' Or *Mrs Dalloway* as a chirpy book that begins: 'Ah! A party tonight! Should be a fine time—fun, friends, nothing stressful, nothing awkward. Should be a blast!' Or Conrad's *Heart of Darkness* as containing: 'Keep hearing about this "unorthodox" Kurtz guy. Sounds interesting. Probably never overtweets about trivialities. My kind of man.' Or, worst of all, John Milton as the poet who wrote in *Paradise Lost*: 'OH MY GOD I'M IN HELL.'

BTW, am I glad that I was born when I was!

Storyteller Sublime

It is the best hour of the day in Jerusalem. The 500-year-old stone walls of the Old City are bathed in the soft warm light of the sinking sun and the evening breeze is a heady mix of the scents of olive, rosemary, sage and lavender. At this hour, Eli Amir, one of Israel's most popular novelists, makes a particularly enchanting raconteur with whom to watch the gently fading light and the emerging silhouettes of domes, towers and steeples.

At seventy-five, but possessed of an enthusiasm and charm that belies his age, he certainly has stories to tell: In 1950, as a boy of thirteen, he fled Baghdad with his Iraqi-Jewish family to the newly formed state of Israel, leaving behind the smells and sounds of what had been home for generations, for an uncertain future. His family struggled in the difficult conditions of an immigrant camp while he bruised his knees in a kibbutz, struggling to break through the racial and ethnic stereotypes in a racial melting pot. Fortunate enough to get a job as a messenger boy, he ferried privileged correspondence in his haversack back and forth from Prime Minister Ben Gurion and often he stood in for the receptionist at the prime minister's house to eavesdrop on history being made in the fledgling state. Schooling himself in Arabic literature and music, he sought to become a bridge between his past and his present, a man with one leg in the East and the other in the West. This Baghdadi Jew, who often refers to himself as ibn Arab (son of an Arab) fulfilled several Civil Service roles, rising from messenger boy to Director General of one of the ministries, and had offers of even higher office. Such was his empathetic ability to talk across communities that he was appointed advisor to the prime minister on Arab issues in East Jerusalem in the wake of the Six Day War in 1967.

The preoccupation of making two ends meet for his immigrant family kept Eli Amir at the bureaucratic desk. But the writer in him had to emerge, the stories had to come bubbling through. So at forty-four, he published his first novel, *The Scapegoat*, the story of a new immigrant teenager from a conservative Middle Eastern background who enters a kibbutz dominated by those from European backgrounds. The clash between new immigrants and old, between two divergent cultures, between the religious and the secular, seen through the eyes of the sensitive young narrator keen to break his shackles but unwilling to deny his roots, spoke to the entire country with an immediacy that made Eli Amir a household name overnight. The novel quickly entered the mainstream canon and became a fixture on the school curriculum.

If *The Scapegoat* was based on Eli Amir's teenage years, the highly accomplished *The Dove Flyer* brings to life the

Baghdad of his childhood. Reading the book, it's easy to believe what Eli Amir's sibling said of him, that young Eli is best recalled as a child sitting at his father's or grandfather's knee, absorbing the stories they had to tell. The novel's thickly populated landscape is layered with stories lived out in the crowded lanes of that once fabled city, where men in navy-blue serge suits sat and played backgammon, smoked hookahs and sipped cardamom-laced coffee. The book depicts the tearing pain of people having to leave the only home they have known in the face of religious discord and politics. But they find that 'running away is no solution. A homeland isn't a hotel that you leave because it's uncomfortable.'

Using straightforward storytelling and eschewing all pedantic pretensions, Amir examines closely issues of identity and the true meaning of exile. We meet people, not unlike the older generation of our own partition-afflicted Punjabi refugees, who spend their lives yearning for the homes they will never see again, that exist only in their dreams. 'There wasn't a day that he didn't go back to Baghdad. This time it was to the oily taste of winter lettuce, the smell of limes, the fresh dates that had melted in his mouth ... Who was it who had once told him that a native land was not a home to be razed, or a rotten tooth to be

pulled out? As if you could extract the earth, the river, the palm trees, the graveyards from a man's heart ...'

But when we begin to talk of the third book, *Yasmine*, Eli Amir's eyes look away into the far distance and his mind seems even further. It took him five years to finish the novel and even then he lingered over it, not wanting to let go of it, because once the book is handed over to editors and publishers, it no longer belongs to the author. Set in East Jerusalem in the immediate aftermath of the Six Day War, *Yasmine* draws heavily on his own experience. The sensitive Arabic-speaking, sympathetic, Jewish advisor, a new immigrant from Iraq—an obvious autobiographical narrator—meets and falls in love with Yasmine, an accomplished, beautiful Palestinian widow who comes back from France, only to go away again. This lyrically depicted love story is at the core of a novel that examines knotty political issues with understanding and sensitivity.

'Is *Yasmine* true?' I ask him, encouraged by the fact that the book is dedicated at least partially to '... Yasmine, wherever you are.'

Eli Amir looks away from the now firm silhouettes of the Old City walls and smiles an inscrutable smile. 'It is all true and it is not true.'

And we leave it at that.

Rage, Rage against the Dying
of the Light

I am in literary legend land in downtown Manhattan, a stone's throw from Greenwich village, New York's answer to the Parisian Left Bank as a home to poets, playwrights and novelists. The village became famous as the stomping ground of figures like Jack Kerouac, William Burroughs, Allen Ginsberg, Dylan Thomas and, in an earlier generation, of Hemingway, Fitzgerald, John Dos Passos and Thomas Wolfe, to name only a handful. It was in its bars, cafés and speakeasies that they created, fought, argued and got drunk.

The iconic Chelsea Hotel is easily recognized by its red brick walls and wrought-iron staircases and balconies. The hotel has closed its lobby to the public at least for a while. Starry-eyed literary fans will not be able to go in and imagine that they heard the strumming of a moody guitar, the declaiming of Benzedrine-inspired verse or the crashing of a bottle against a wall. They can at best stand on the sidewalk under the scaffolding and look at the various plaques that are fixed outside the hotel in memory of some of its most famous residents, including Arthur Miller, Thomas Wolfe, Leonard Cohen, Arthur C. Clarke.

But the one that catches and holds the eye is the one about the Welsh poet, Dylan Thomas. It is simple but hugely evocative: 'Dylan Thomas lived and wrote at the Chelsea hotel and from here he sailed out to die.'

Light breaks where no sun shines;/where no sea runs, the waters of the heart/Push in their tides; ... I have surreptitiously lifted these lines from one of Thomas's poems to use as an epigraph for my collection of short stories. They serve my purpose well, succinctly capturing the mysterious nature of the human heart. I feel I owe him one and there seems no better way of returning the favour than by following the path down which he sailed out to die.

So late that night, with only a few wispy clouds escorting a three-quarter moon over the Manhattan sky, I trace Dylan Thomas's steps as he walks to his favourite watering hole, the White Horse Tavern, that claims its birth in 1880. It was not only *his* favourite hangout. Writers like Anais Nin, James Baldwin, Norman Mailer, Bob Dylan, Jim Morrison and Jack Kerouac draped themselves around the bar often enough and it is said that the drunk Kerouac was bounced out of the tavern on many occasions. In fact, he mentions in his novel *Desolation Angels* that he found the words 'Go home, Kerouac' scribbled in the toilet there. But it is Dylan Thomas who has claimed this tavern as his own, referring to it lovingly as 'The Horse', enamoured no doubt by its British pub atmosphere reminiscent of home.

The café occupies a prominent corner, standing out with its old-fashioned tin roof and white horses emblazoned across several signs. Joyous groups crowd the tables under an ornate false ceiling, which contrasts with the tables and floors of unpolished rough wood. Dylan Thomas memorabilia is strewn all around in the form of brass plaques, quotations, sketches. A spectral legend seems to drift in and out of conversations and then proceeds to stand at the bar, resting its chin on one elbow: did Dylan Thomas really come here, drink eighteen straight whiskies and simply die, it seems to mockingly ask the crowd.

I confront the waitress with the plummy London accent with the question. With practised ease she sits down across the table and relates in a tone that is honest and straightforward: 'You will find as many stories as narrators. Some say eighteen whiskies, others say twelve, but I think it was twelve.' I dig for more details. What was the whisky he drank? 'Jamesons,' she replies promptly. That's a detail I have never come across in various versions of the tale.

It was 1953 and Dylan Thomas was on his fourth tour of America under the guidance of his agent John Brinnin. He was at the height of his powers as well as his popularity, conducting well-attended readings and selling as much, if not more, than T.S. Eliot. He was also holding rehearsals for his play *Under Milk Wood*, which would later star Richard Burton and be highly acclaimed. But he was also seriously ill, with the New York smog exacerbating his chest condition; his excessive drinking and smoking hardly helped matters. One night he inexplicably left his American mistress Liz Reteill at the Chelsea at two in the morning and walked out towards The White Horse. Over two hours there he downed several large whiskies, and we will let the historians continue to quibble whether it was eighteen or twelve. Suffice it to say that the number was large and beyond a point it really doesn't matter. He then returned to the hotel, where he is said to have boasted to Liz, 'I've had eighteen straight whiskies. I think that's the record.'

The next afternoon he and Liz returned to the tavern, where he ordered the hair of the dog to help him tide over his inevitable hangover. It was only when he returned to the hotel that he took to his bed. His condition worsened, and by the time he was moved to St Vincent's hospital, he was comatose. His wife Caitlin arrived a couple of days later; understandably, her first question to his agent was: 'Well, is the bloody man dead yet?'

A few days later he was indeed dead, probably not from the impact of the Jamesons alone but also his underlying condition; pneumonia, pressure on the brain and a fatty liver was the official diagnosis, but medical negligence was also rumoured. It was the whisky story, however, that stuck, in keeping as it was with Thomas's image of a 'doomed poet'.

He was only thirty-nine and he certainly went on his way with a flourish, following his own advice that he had fashioned for his dying father in his best-known lines:

> Do not go gentle into that good night,
> Old age should burn and rave at close of day;
> Rage, rage against the dying of the light.

E.M. Forster Chews 'Paan'

Occasional writing is a much neglected and sometimes denigrated genre probably because of the misperception that it is a hold-all for an author's leftovers or a brave attempt by a friendly editor to milk an author's notebooks for the last possible paragraph. More often than not, these occasional pieces—essays, musings, poems, sketches, memoirs, recollections—turn out to be little gems. Inspiration need not always work itself out into a novel or even a short story, as is evident in the burgeoning blogging industry. Additionally, the reader has a huge advantage when he picks up a collection of occasional writings: he can dip in where he wants and surface when he likes.

And so it was with *Abinger Harvest*, a collection of about eighty pieces chosen by E.M. Forster from his contributions to various periodicals, all written before the Second World War. This 1946 reprint, picked off a London street, is a so-called 'cheap' edition, cloth-bound in lovely bright orange, covered with a self-effacing grey jacket; why did anyone ever call these editions 'cheap'? I skirt politely past the essays on the English character, and the ones on the passing events of the mid-War years, and those analysing the various diversions of a dying empire. Promising myself that someday I would return to them, I resist the section on writers: Forster's views on Conrad and T.E. Lawrence, Virginia Woolf and Ibsen, T.S. Eliot and Proust. I am trying to find my passage to India through the book and I do not want to be waylaid.

I am not disappointed. In the last section of the book Forster salutes the Orient at Egypt, muses on mosques and museums, tips his hat towards Babur, once 'a robber boy, sorely in need of advice ... scuttling over the highlands of Central Asia'. This was a Central Asia in which his two ancestors, Timur and Genghiz Khan, 'had produced between them so numerous a progeny that a frightful congestion of royalties had resulted along the upper waters of the Jaxartes and the Oxus, and in Afghanistan. One could scarcely travel two miles without being held up by an Emperor.' Skimming lightly through these pieces I arrive with Forster at the borders of India.

In a little nugget of a piece, Forster describes a visit to Ujjain in search of the ruins of Vikramaditya's palace in the dusty plain with its shady groves of trees, random groups of villagers, meandering, unhasty rural tracks. He evokes Kalidasa and Shakuntala and stands ankle-deep in the churning water of the Shipra which 'gave nothing to the land; no meadows or water weeds edged it. It flowed, like the Ganges of legend, precipitate out of heaven across earth on its way to plunge under the sea and purify hell.' Forster then celebrates Jodhpur, 'the land of heroism, where deeds which would have been brutal elsewhere have been touched with glory.' In other incisive pieces he discusses two books by Tagore, the Arjuna–Krishna dialogue on the battlefield and the mind of the Indian princes, seen as allies by the British Government of India 'as its own troubles grow and a Gandhi succeeds to a Tilak.'

But my favourite piece emerges when Forster comes 'in the silence of the noontide heat ... to a secluded glade among low, scrub-covered hills' and finds there a straw-padded enclosure with twines that are 'aromatic and lush, with heart-shaped leaves that yearn towards the sun and thrive in the twilight of their aspirations, trained across lateral strings into a subtle and complicated symphony.' There are men 'naked and manure-coloured' tending to each delicate tendril and he wonders: 'What acolytes, serving what nameless deity?'

The deity, as he finds out when he eats a leaf and his 'tongue is stabbed by a hot and angry orange in alliance with pepper', is none other than Pan, as he spells it. The humble paan or betel leaf made a surprisingly strong impact on early visitors to the East, including Marco Polo and Duarte

Barbosa, a sixteenth-century Portuguese official in Cochin. Barbosa wrote that in India, the betel 'is habitually chewed by both men and women, night and day, in public places and roads by day, and in bed by night, so that their chewing thereof has no pause ... It makes the mouth red and the teeth black.' Rather succinctly put!

Forster is critical of Anglo-India, which did not take to paan, regarding its consumption filthy and so un-British. He praises the role paan plays in Indian society: it is a 'nucleus for hospitality, and much furtive intercourse takes place under its little shield. One can "go to a Pan", "give a Pan", and so on: less compromising than giving a party, and on to the Pan tea, coffee, ices, sandwiches, sweets, and whisky-sodas can be tacked.' He also alludes to an 'allowance for Pan' (but omits the bidi) which is a delicate reference to pin-money. Descriptions of 'Pan's trinity' of ingredients—betel, lime, areca—follow, of which the lime is the 'least honourable'. Areca, or supari, reminds Forster of iron pyrites and can be alarming when first tasted, but one can get nicely used to it. Cardamom seeds, he observes, are sometimes added and the whole can then be folded up either in the manner of 'billet-doux' or fastened at an angle with a clove.

The paan, he instructs, should never be bitten into but taken as a whole and the consequences awaited. The novice when he feels the iron pyrites going under the tongue 'rises in disorder, rushes in panic to the courtyard, and spatters shrapnel over bystanders; it is as if the whole mineral kingdom has invaded him under a vegetable veil, for simultaneously the lime starts stinging'. But if he perseveres, then heavenly peace ensues as 'the ingredients salute each other, a single sensation is established, and Pan, without ceasing to be a problem, becomes a pleasure. The cardamoms crack, the formidable areca yields, splinters vainly takes refuge in the interstices of the gums, and is gone. Warm and cleanly, one's mouth beats in tune with the infinite, while the harmony, moving within, slowly establishes its reign ...'

But if one looks into the mirror, it's another matter. The result is bright red, inexplicable with green betel, the brown areca and the white lime. There is the danger that 'one may forget, go to play bridge at the Club with vermillion jaws and be ruined forever'. Indians, Forster says, who eat paan all the time get red permanently and their teeth blacken: 'Their looks are against them, but their breath is sweet'. There follows a detailed description of the serving of paan, including the various kinds of paan daan or boxes—compartmentalized, circular, rectangular, storeyed, Bidar-made with silver inlay and so on. And a sensuous description of an Indian hostess making a paan—choosy, gracious, whimsical, mysterious. But don't get me wrong: Forster does not want this to be a foray into the mystery of the East. 'Pan' is for all humanity.

The next time I set out for an after-dinner stroll in the fragrant Delhi summer night to the neighbourhood paan shop, I will pause a moment before I decide between a meetha or a saada paan. According to Forster, there is also the 'Comic Pan', which contains salt and is given to buffoons, and a 'Tragic Pan', which contains ground glass and is given to enemies.

The Unquiet Englishman

An early Saturday morning walk past the old gun, rusting on a cliff for half a century or more, pointing at some imaginary target far above the foaming waves with the gunner's seat still turned to a convenient angle, puts me, for no obvious reason, in a mood to read Graham Greene. To read at a stretch some strangely detached and yet very intricately plotted story of men in remote corners of the world, men with an unresolved past picking their way across a moral landscape infested with the landmines of betrayal and jealousy, alienated men working out their own private deals with God, their hard-boiled cynicism disguising some sentimental core. A story about some drink-driven foreign correspondent or death-seeking traveller or whimsical spy in a pastel suit whose only obvious loyalty is to the cocktail hour.

The Quiet American seems to push itself out towards my hand. Partly because I read somewhere recently that Pico Iyer regards it as a sort of private Bible (and I will try not to reproduce his reasons here) and partly because the copy I possess is a very readable edition brought out for the Greene Centennial in 2004, printed on thick creamy paper, with an attractively rough, almost unfinished edge. Both a tortured love entanglement and prescient political history, the novel successfully documented the anti-colonialist impulse and the beginnings of the Vietnam War, to the point that it became essential reading during the war itself, with foreign correspondents gifting copies to each other.

The book's story unfolds like an accordion in the hands of a master: A cynical, opium-smoking British journalist, Fowler, lives in an adulterous liaison with a beautiful local girl, Phuong, in Saigon of the early fifties, when the French were unsuccessfully fighting Ho Chi Minh. Pyle, a younger American, idealistic and dangerously innocent, bumbles onto the scene; he also falls in love with Phuong and takes her away from Fowler, though in a strangely honourable way. Fowler is the hardened professional, refusing to take sides; he is, as he says, a reporter, not a leader writer. Pyle, on the other hand, is well-intentioned but destructive in his action, finally murderous. Phuong is a deliberately underdeveloped character, a beautiful metaphor of the mysterious East, exploited by the foreigners and yet somehow out of reach, never quite understood. She was 'the hiss of steam, the clink of a cup, she was a certain hour of the night and the promise of rest'. The fast-paced and tight plot, bolstered by evocative and moody descriptions, plays out against several themes—the old colonialism and the new American way, religion, love, desire and guilt.

To say more on the actual story may spoil it for those who have not yet read it. Better instead to focus on two surrounding aspects. First, the impact of Greene's personal life on the novel: In 1947, Greene had separated from his long-suffering wife Vivien, though they would remain married till his death in 1991. While living with his mistress Dorothy Glover, he had also begun an affair with a wealthy married woman, Catherine Walston (the 'C' to whom *The End of the Affair* is dedicated), who would remain the grand passion of his life. He was, however, unable to persuade her to leave her husband. Their meetings became limited and more difficult and that was at least one of the reasons why Greene travelled to Malaya and Indo-China and tried, unsuccessfully as it turned out, to forget his personal torment by throwing himself in danger's way and seeking relief in opium. Much of this is reflected in Fowler's life—a mirror for many of Greene's own beliefs and traits—in the book. His last farewell to Vivien, when she watched him walk away from the house, looking back but not waving, is also one of the memories that Fowler sifts through: 'My wife's face at a window when I came home to say goodbye for the last time.' Even the letter that Fowler writes to his wife in England, seeking divorce so that he can marry Phuong, could be one that Greene himself wrote to Vivien and the wife's response is one that he may have imagined to be Vivien's.

Saigon captivated Greene: 'The spell was first cast ... by the tall elegant girls in white silk trousers, by the pewter evening light on flat paddy fields, where the water-buffaloes trudged fetlock-deep with a slow primeval gait ... the Chinese gambling houses in Cholon, above all by that feeling of exhilaration that a measure of danger brings.' He haunted the Majestic and Continental hotels on the rue Catinat with its cafés and bars, where much of the book's action happens. He visited the brothels and opium dens, travelled across the war-torn country with French patrols, 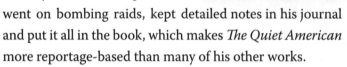 went on bombing raids, kept detailed notes in his journal and put it all in the book, which makes *The Quiet American* more reportage-based than many of his other works.

The other aspect is the book's avowed anti-Americanism, most vividly demonstrated by the fact that in 1956, the Soviet newspaper *Pravda* gratefully hailed, across five columns, the novel as a major event in British literary history that demonstrated the naïve and murderous impact of America's anti-communism. (This was in turn ridiculed by *Newsweek* under the headline 'When Greene is Red.') Greene, belonging to the British elite, had a sentimental, almost paternalistic attachment to the so-called Third World and resented the increasing and inevitable American presence, regarding it as naïve and uncultured. He nurtured nostalgia, according to Anthony Burgess, 'for the Rider Haggard, Conan Doyle, John Buchan hero pursuing the cause of British decency in some fever-ridden outpost'. His visceral anger at what he regarded as dangerous American innocence in stepping into settings without understanding them, as well as his dislike for American traits and culture, runs through the book like a caustic gash. 'Innocence,' says Fowler in the book, 'is like a dumb leper who has lost his bell, wandering the world, meaning no harm.' He is tired of 'the whole pack of them with their private stores of Coca-Cola and their portable hospitals and their too wide cars and their not quite latest guns'. He didn't want Pyle to be messing around Indo-China supplying explosives that ended up killing innocents in the name of democracy; rather he wanted to see him 'reading the Sunday supplements at home and following baseball ... safe with a standardized American girl who subscribed to a Book Club'. Naturally, such criticism was not well received in the US and Greene's attitude was ascribed to personal pique at not having been given a visa because of a few weeks of membership in the communist party in 1922. *The New Yorker*, while mocking Greene, accidentally, and unkindly, touched off another theory: That Pyle, the American, was actually a thinly disguised Englishman—'a naïve chap who speaks bad French, eats tasteless food and is only accidentally and episodically heterosexual.'

Come to think of it, Pyle's insistence on fairness, honour, the right thing and 'playing it straight' does sound more British public school than anything else. Isn't playing it straight a cricketing phrase, after all?

Of Lords, Aunts and Pigs

For the last few days, P.G. Wodehouse has been happening to me. I mean to say, I knew he was around all these years, sitting sagely on that treasured shelf, smiling his genial knowing smile and smoking his pipe. Every once in a while, when the heart was inordinately burdened, he would push across one of his books. I would read a few pages reverently and having achieved instant relief from the moment's predicament would put it back gently and gratefully. But of late I seem to find him at every corner, whispering 'pssst' as I go past or what-ho-ing to me across crowded streets. The Master is insistent on renewing our acquaintance. It's been too long, he seems to say. Or perhaps it's just his way of removing any dark shadow that may hover momentarily over his fans—the timely pick-me-up, not unlike the one administered by Jeeves to Bertie on the morning after the bender in town. So he's been turning up at unexpected times in the least expected places until it has begun to feel like the old times, when he would constantly be in my bag, or under my pillow, guiding me through his wondrous world of pigs and Lords, butlers and goofs, aunts and country houses.

First, it was his cricket book, *Wodehouse at the Wicket*. No connection with this IPL business. Wodehouse would have frowned at the dashed thing. The absence of white and the over-abundance of chorus girls, or what passes for chorus girls these days, would have been enough to send him tut-tutting all the way back to the pavilion. The book was thoughtfully slipped into my bag by my son before a flight, having given up pushing sci-fi or fantasy tomes which he now knows I have neither the mind to read nor the heart to refuse. This one was a winner; a better way to spend five hours in a transit lounge has not been invented. Murray Hedgcock, the cricket historian, had put together several of Wodehouse's cricket tales and, in a perceptive introduction, traced the writer's lifelong deep passion for the game.

Primarily a fast bowler and a doubtful bat, often batting at number ten and scoring regulation ducks, Wodehouse played for the Dulwich team, including against the

MCC. Post his school years, he would often take the P.G. Wodehouse XI to play against his old school and engage in some light-hearted cricket but he had already moved from playing to writing about the game, including books known to our generation as *Mike at Wrykin* and *Mike and Psmith*, which first appeared under different titles. Yet he played as many as six times at Lord's when the venue was made available for modest-level matches such as Authors vs Actors, the authors' team being captained by none other than Sir Arthur Conan Doyle. In another match the Authors played against Publishers (imagine that: take this bouncer for the missed royalty cheque!). The most invaluable nugget contained in the book traces the origin of the name Jeeves to Percy Jeeves, a Warwickshire professional cricketer known for his impeccable grooming, smart shirts and spotlessly clean flannels. Wodehouse probably saw him take a couple of smooth, effortless catches in a match between Gloucestershire and Warwickshire. The name, the immaculate appearance and silent efficiency stuck and the inimitable manservant appeared first in 1916, just weeks after the original Percy Jeeves died in the war in France.

After the cricket book, I chanced upon the *Paris Review* interviews, a long-running series of leisurely, in-depth interviews with writers through the decades. The *Review* caught up with Wodehouse when he was 'ninety-one and a half', as he pointed out to the interviewer. He had just finished *Bachelors Anonymous* and was thrilled to bits with it, wondering how he would ever top it. He didn't want to end up like Bernard Shaw, turning out awful stuff in his nineties. Shaw, incidentally, knew that the stuff was awful, but couldn't stop writing. Wodehouse felt he had slowed down a bit, doing only a thousand words a day, finishing a novel in six or seven months. The interview reveals the hard work behind the seemingly effortless, breezy final product: 400 pages of notes for each book, detailed plot and scene construction, endless revision, morning to evening, seven days a week. Again, several gems turn up: Psmith was the only major character taken from real life; Galahad was a sort of grown-up Psmith; Jeeves was intended for one-time use with two speaking lines.

Wodehouse comes across as a man totally happy with the writer's life. 'I know I was writing stories when I was five,' he says. 'I don't remember what I did before that. Just loafed, I suppose.' In fact he did nothing else but write except for a short stint at the Hong Kong and Shanghai Bank where the 'idea of going to Bombay or somewhere and being a branch manager and being paid in rupees' scared him stiff and he left after, of course, having written a story in a new bank ledger. There were the early struggles of literary life when the wolf was always at the door and he felt that he was being constantly chased by 'little men with black beards'. But soon the *Saturday Evening Post* accepted to serialize *Something New* for $3500 and the cash register rang louder and louder after that. We also learn that he carefully read all his reviews, enjoyed other humorists like Perelman and Thurber and thought that Somerset Maugham was constantly unhappy and unpleasant.

Scarcely had I finished reading the interview than a book of literary anecdotes came to hand. Here I must admit I looked for Wodehouse and found this delightful snippet. An old lady sitting next to him at dinner raved about his work and told him how her sons had piles of his books and read each one as it came out. Then she chirped: 'And when I tell them that I have actually been sitting at dinner with Edgar Wallace, I don't know what they will say.'

And finally, there is this life-saver, an internet resource called the Random Wodehouse Quote Generator brought to you by none other than the Drones Club. It pops out one Wodehouse quotation at a time. Take one per day, preferably on an empty stomach, and the world will appear a much happier place. This is the one I drew this morning: 'Jeeves lugged my purple socks out of the drawer as if he were a vegetarian fishing a caterpillar out of his salad.'

Of Writers and writers

Judging simply from the amount of time they have at their disposal for putting pen to paper, writers can be divided broadly into two categories.

The first category could be called Writers, with a capital W. These are the recipients of those mythical-sized advances, sometimes with the first book itself, sold by an angel in the human form of a literary agent. Film contracts, translations into twenty-five languages, three-book deals quickly follow. Life is a breezy rush from one literary festival to the next, interspersed with interviews, appearances on the lecture circuit, research trips for the next book. Of course, if the success is to be sustained, a huge amount of work has to be done and they must retreat to their desks to do it, because there really is no other way. These full-time writers then develop their personalized writing routines, which also equip them to answer with complete authority when wide-eyed fans ask questions like, Do you write in the morning or evening? With a pen or on the computer? Wearing airline socks or bare feet on cold marble? They can give convincing answers from real life about how they gather the energy that goes into their books, how they persevere, how they prepare, how they rewrite ... each in his own way, with music or silence, with coffee or gin, at dawn or midnight.

Simone de Beauvoir, for instance, would work from ten to one and then again from five to nine and find time to see Sartre every evening or lunchtime. C.S. Lewis would be at his desk at nine after breakfast at eight and work through till one. After lunch at precisely one, he would be out for a walk at two, usually with a friend whom he didn't need to talk to. Tea would be waiting when he returned at exactly 4.15 and he would drink it in solitude. Then back to work from five to seven in the evening. James Thurber, who had severe eyesight problems, would spend the morning rolling the text over in his mind and then dictate 2,000 words to a secretary in the afternoon. Of course he would continue to write in his head even in company and his wife had to come up to him in the middle of parties and say: 'Damn it, Thurber, stop writing.' Gunter Grass would start at ten after a long breakfast with music and then carry on till one, stop for a coffee break, and go on till seven in the evening. Hemingway would begin writing at first light and go on until he came 'to a place where you still have your juice and you know what will happen next and you stop and try to live through until the next day when you hit it again ... Nothing can hurt you, nothing can happen, nothing means anything until the next day when you do it again. It is the wait until the next day that is hard to get through.' Haruki Murakami works from four in the morning to lunch and then trains for marathons in the afternoon, convinced that the writing of novels needs mental as well as physical strength. Amos Oz once told me that he walks into the desert in the early morning to absorb its silences and this keeps him going during those long hours at his desk.

By now you get the idea. These Writers have a tough life, for nothing finally comes easy, but they don't need to go to office at nine to do a job and bring in the monthly cheque that will keep the wolf from the door.

But what of those who write between things, let us call them the lower-case writers. These are the ones with a day job, which may even be an interesting and demanding one. These are the desperate jugglers of two worlds who cannot help a rueful smile when they look at the advance offered by the publisher and are reconciled to the fact that write they must, even though their annual royalty will never add up to one tank full of gas per month, or buy basketball shoes for two kids in the same financial year. So they slog away at the day job, writing early morning or late nights, on weekends or on trains, or in their head Thurber-like, all the time waiting for the silver bullet. Lest they lose heart, it would be nice to recall some famous names who had to do this, at least for a while, a fact that is being documented by some literary journals now.

P.G. Wodehouse worked two years at the Hong Kong and Shanghai Bank and learned to hate it until he was well known enough to leave and bring out his first book, *The Pothunters*. But he did use the banking experience for *Psmith in the City*. T.S. Eliot worked at the Lloyds Bank for eight years and, craving financial security, actually liked it. Despite efforts by Ezra Pound and others to 'free' him, he continued to work there even after fame had touched his shoulder with her magic wand and he was known as the writer of *Prufrock* and *The Wasteland*, in which, incidentally, he used scenes he saw on his way to work. When he did resign, the reason he gave was 'domestic anxieties', which meant his wife's deteriorating health and not the need for more time to write. John Grisham, a lawyer, would get up at 5.00 a.m. and be at his office with a yellow legal pad before him by 5.30. He would write one page a day, whether it took him ten minutes or two hours and then turn to his day job. Anthony Trollope worked as a postal surveyor for a long stretch of his writing life. Travelling around England, America and Ireland on work, he would take along his folding desk to write his novels. He would work from 5.30 to 8.30 a.m. with a watch in front of him, set on producing 250 words every fifteen minutes. No wonder he wrote forty-nine novels in thirty-five years. Kafka wrote several books while working as chief legal secretary at the Workmans' Accident Insurance Institute and obviously picked up enough on the dehumanizing impact of bureaucracy at his job. William Faulkner was a postmaster at the University of Mississippi but would get off to play a round of golf in the afternoons and write poems, later gathered in *The Marble Fawn*. Kurt Vonnegut sold cars, managing a Saab dealership on Cape Cod. Sylvia Plath, tellingly, worked as a receptionist at a psychiatric hospital. Jack London was an oyster pirate, raiding farms and selling oysters in the Oakland market to make ends meet. And somehow the books kept coming.

So soldier on, all ye who work at day and write at night.

The Writer in Winter

Somewhat embarrassedly, I must admit that I had not read Paul Auster, widely acknowledged as one of America's leading novelists, till his *Winter Journal* recently came to hand. Perhaps the *Journal* is not the best book with which to start exploring a writer who is more often than not characterized as 'inventive' and known for his ability to delve deep into the dilemmas of an isolated soul. Perhaps one should have started with a famous novel like *The New York Trilogy* or the highly acclaimed early memoir, *The Invention of Solitude*, books which may better demonstrate Auster's mastery of the patterns of the American urban landscape or his romance with the curious workings of coincidence and chance, those unexpected by-lanes that suddenly appear and change human lives forever. But then, as I said, it was *Winter Journal* that came to hand. It seemed a slim, easily readable first book and besides, its first paragraph was irresistible bait: 'You think it will never happen to you, that it cannot happen to you, that you are the only person in the world to whom none of these things will ever happen, and then, one by one they all begin to happen to you, in the same way they happen to everyone else.'

Thus, in second-person narrative, begins this introspective meditation on ageing and the ravages of time on mind, body and soul as Auster marks his sixty-fourth birthday, 'inching ever closer to senior citizenship, to the days of Medicare and Social Service benefits, to a time when more and more of your friends would have left you'. In other words, he is about to enter the winter of his life, the time when he is asking himself: 'How many mornings are left?' When each of us approaches this inevitable season of our lives, we no doubt find our own devices to meet it, one hand outstretched. Auster's reaction is to look back and remember and catalogue: 'Speak now before it is too late, and then hope to go on speaking until there is nothing more to be said. Time is running out, after all. Perhaps it is just as well to put aside your stories for now and try to examine what it has felt like to live inside this body from the first day you can remember being alive until this one. A catalogue of sensory data. What one might call a phenomenology of breathing.'

With a self-obsessed honesty—which is perhaps the only way it can be done—Auster sets out recollections of pains and pleasures in a manner to which any thinking individual, given to looking within himself, can relate to. Memories of early childhood when one is physically so near the 'little world of crawling ants and lost coins, of fallen twigs and dented bottle caps, of dandelions and clover ... (and) armies of ants travelling in and out of their powdery hills'. Of scars acquired one by one; the stitches on the cheek, the cut on the chin, the split eyebrows. And these brought to mind my own, each with its painful story—the forehead split when the corner of a fireplace came in the way; the toe that was nearly torn off by barbed wire when I ran after a floating kite; the way the skinned knee went chalk-white before the blood began to seep into it after my bike skidded on a stony rough road. And the scars on the heart caused by 'how many infatuations and crushes, how many ardours and pursuits, how many mad surges and desires'.

Paul Auster admits to being a willing slave of Eros and talks freely of the women he loved before his final—and obviously blissful—marriage to the writer Siri Hustvedt, 'each one different from the others, some round and some lean, some short and some tall, some bookish and some athletic, some moody and some outgoing ...' attracted all the time by 'the inner light ... the spark of singularity ... the blaze of revealed selfhood'. In fact, the search for sexual pleasure and its memories fuels a significant part of the *Journal*, as the young Auster, living in a 'torment of frustration and never-ending sexual arousal', seeks to lose his virginity in relatively prudish America of the early 1960s, and finally does so unsatisfactorily in a brothel. More charming is his encounter with a Parisian prostitute who recites Baudelaire to him during a magical night.

Auster employs an interesting device to recall memories: the use of his twenty-one 'permanent addresses', the houses he stayed in until he moved to the Brooklyn brownstone where he settled, determined to stay there 'until you can no longer crawl up and down the stairs, until they carry you out and put you in your grave'. Each house brings back its time and age, its friends and visitors, its ghosts and hallucinations. As do the descriptions of incessant travel and the unreal existence between 'the here of home and the there of somewhere else'. And so we are told of the agony and folly of his first marriage, the made-in-heaven second marriage, the car crash in which his carelessness nearly killed his family, the false heart attack that was a swollen oesophagus.

The most evocative parts of the book revolve around the deaths of his divorced parents. Numbed by the death of his mother, Auster holds on to his bottle of Oban whisky and finally dissolves on the floor in a crippling panic attack. He then recalls his mother's life with affection and understanding, evocatively outlining the three persons that dwelt in her one body—the dazzling, charming diva; the responsible, solid, competent, generous businesswoman; and the helpless, anxious, debilitated, neurotic hypochondriac, afraid of elevators, airplanes, open spaces. The sudden death of his father years earlier, on a snow-bound January night, left behind 'a feeling of unfinished business, the hollow frustration of words not spoken, of opportunities missed forever'. That death coincided with the end of Auster's first marriage as well as with 'an epiphanic moment of clarity that pushed you through a crack in the universe and allowed you to start writing again'. This moment, the second beginning of Paul Auster as a writer, came as he watched a group of dancers on a New York stage, while his father was dying somewhere else—'the ghoulish trigonometry of fate'.

Auster calls writing a lesser form of dance. 'One foot forward, and then the other foot forward, the double drumbeat of your heart ... Writing begins in the body, it is the music of the body, and even if the words have meaning, can sometimes have meaning, the music of the words is where the meanings begin. You sit at your desk in order to write down the words, but in your head you are still walking, always walking, and what you hear is the rhythm of your heart, the beating of your heart.'

Self-indulgent at times, narcissistic on occasion, the *Winter Journal* leaves itself open to criticism. But it has done the trick: I will end up reading more Paul Auster.

Remembrances of Things Past

The rain pours down. The glowering grey of the clouds thickens the green of the neem, the jamun, even the keekar trees of Delhi. Traffic grinds to a halt; all manner of cars show that they are capable of stalling. Little rivers with a hundred rainbows swirling in them flow swiftly down the sides of the glistening roads.

Memories of monsoons past glisten in these flowing rainbows. Childhood monsoons in a very green valley when the sky cracked up in a way it no longer does and little paper boats went tossing down the bricked drain that ran outside our gate. When lights had to be put on at noon in school classrooms and nothing could be heard but the drumming of the rain on the corrugated iron roof and on the way home we let the rain wash us down, invincible in our raincoats and gum boots. Youthful monsoons when we dodged from one dripping tree to another down university lanes, crossed arms protecting original certificates in flimsy cellophane folders and a rose that drifted from the hand of a leaning beauty into a fast forming puddle could have been the beginning of a romance that never went anywhere. Bombay monsoons when the rain lashed my Marine Drive window with apocalyptic force and a sea of black umbrellas came onto the streets and we extended our office lunches in the gentrified Irani restaurant just to ponder the mystery of the cold, unsmiling visage of the owner's daughter as she stood behind the counter, counting coins.

Press the monsoon button in the mind and these memories inevitably appear, their colours untarnished with time. But how true are these memories to what actually happened and are they really shared by anyone else in exactly the same way? How many classmates of mine from that school under the pines remember the way the raincoat stuck to your arms when you tried to take it off? Does that leaning beauty ever think of the rose that drifted unknowing from her hand into a puddle? And what does that nameless girl behind the counter recall of those monsoons, certainly not two callow youngsters who wouldn't get up from the corner table? Not just monsoons—the same applies to memories of people, of relationships, of regrets, emotional debts, guilt, anger, all stored up from the past and left to solidify through the passage of time.

Such questions of memory and time, and the tricks they play with each other, are examined masterfully in *The Sense of an Ending*, a slim gem of a book by Julian Barnes. 'What you end up remembering,' says Barnes's narrator, 'isn't always the same as what you have witnessed' and what we carry with us towards the end of our lives whether they be visions of misty monsoons or long-ago broken hearts may actually only be 'approximate memories which time has deformed into certainty'. The young can predict to a large extent the pains and tribulations that ageing is likely to bring—loneliness, divorce, death, loss of status, loss of desire and desirability. But they usually cannot imagine themselves looking back from a vantage point in the future, with the advantage of new emotions that only time brings. They cannot imagine how their view of the past will evolve, how a remembered scene will dissolve and reform, until it again finally settles into something permanent. As one ages, the entire process becomes even more unreliable as more and more witnesses to one's past fall by the wayside and 'there is less corroboration, and therefore less certainty, as to what you are or have been'. The thought is disturbing.

The book has a deceptively simple storyline—which I am not about to reveal in its entirety—but successfully plumbs impressive emotional depths. The narrator, Tony Webster, a retired, quietly divorced man, has memories of his youth with which he is comfortable—memories of a clique of intellectually pretentious friends, a girlfriend, a weekend spent with her family, a suicide or two—all of which he is now reconciled to and has slotted into permanent pigeon-holes with the right amount of attachment, of affection, admiration, regret and guilt. Then suddenly, a letter from a lawyer informing him of a strange bequest upends all this. It reopens assessments of relationships and events, the why and wherefore of life that he had neatly tied up and left in the warehouse of the past. A letter he wrote forty years ago is given back to him: he finds his younger self standing before him, and it is not a pleasant image. He realizes that time can confuse and confound. It can inject doubts and questions into what we always thought to be certainties and make them wobble before our very eyes. He begins to recall forgotten details and replays familiar images, holding them up to the light, twisting and turning them to see if they actually meant something different than what he had always assumed. Slowly the past begins to transform, motives change, new causalities appear and relationships are reformulated. In short, a new reality replaces that vision which memory had always believed to be true. He realizes that 'when we are young, we invent different futures for ourselves; when we are old, we invent different pasts for others'. And often these inventions do not hold. Memory is simply not events plus time; often it may turn out to be what we have forgotten. Time doesn't always 'act as a fixative, rather as a solvent'.

Which leads me to another half-forgotten thought that today doesn't sound as glib as it did in one's youth: It's not time that is passing, my friend, it's you and I who are passing.

Poems on the Sand

Some half a century ago, Paula Ben-Gurion, wife of Israel's first prime minister, looked over the hedge while pottering around her Tel Aviv garden and espied a young man. She invited him in and a chance encounter became a calling. The young man was Clinton Bailey, a Jewish American who had been raised in upstate New York and had come to Israel in search of his destiny. A teaching job at Ben-Gurion's kibbutz at Sde Boker in the Negev soon followed where Bailey came in close touch with the Bedouin of the desert, their ancient culture already fraying under the inexorable influence of the forces of modernism. For the next four decades and more, Bailey studied the Bedouin of the Negev and the Sinai, lived with them months at a time, become their trusted friend, and a devoted witness to the passing of a way of life that has survived in the desert since pre-Biblical times.

By the time I met Bailey, he was acknowledged as the foremost expert on Bedouin history, culture, poetry and law. Many enriching encounters ensued, culminating in a day-long tour with him in the Negev desert, eating with the Bedouin from a common platter heaped with rice and chicken and drinking strong bitter coffee cooked over coals in a hole in the sand, never mind that many of the tents were now of cement sheets and ramshackle cars jostled with camels in the compound.

One would assume that an unlettered nomadic culture that devoted its energies to sheer survival in the inhospitable desert would not lend itself naturally to the fine art of poetry. Bailey's monumental work *Bedouin Poetry from Sinai and the Negev* turns this perception on its head and shows that survival is not only economic but also social, spiritual, psychological and aesthetic. Poetry was for the Bedouin a counter to the stark harshness of the desert: it served as an expression of emotion as well as a practical way of passing a message, easier to remember since it was in rhyme. It was also a vehicle for celebrating traditional Bedouin traits—extreme generosity, hospitality, bravery and honour.

Over two decades, from 1967 to 1988, Bailey recorded 700 Bedouin poems recited around desert campfires. Some of these would be recited by the poet himself (known as *shair* in Arabic, as in Urdu); others would be those written by revered poets from earlier generations and committed to memory by reciters and travellers, a practice that ensured that a popular poem would travel huge distances from the deserts of Arabia to the Negev and Sinai, or into Iraq and Syria. The present book contains 113 of these poems, chosen primarily for their popularity among the Bedouin. Each poem has a short introductory essay explaining its context and myriad, enlightening footnotes that are testimony to Bailey's sincerity of commitment and academic discipline.

Divided into sections based on the basic motives of Bedouin poetry—emotion, communication, instruction and entertainment—the book also contains an exciting selection from the eight-year exchange of poems between Anez Abu Salim and other Bedouin. The free-spirited Anez, besides being the finest living poet in Sinai, was also a leading smuggler bringing income to hundreds of Bedouin and had been locked up by the Egyptians. His poems express his pessimism and despair in prison as well as his pain at finding out that two of his wives had proved to be unfaithful. He is informed of their indiscretions by another poet who writes:

Tell Anez that with relish they eat what he's sown
A harvest of darkened-eyed girls he'd once known.

In the end, Anez divorced all three wives to avoid further calumny and wrote:

> And, lest every Zed and Abed laugh at me,
> I've set my three non-bearing she-camels free.

Anez also wrote many other types of poems, including one to King Husein when he was not allowed to meet him by Mubarak (Had the luck of Husein and myself so conspired/A meeting of worthies would have transpired). And another, full of gentle flattery, to King Abdullah of Jordan in the hope of being presented a fine camel.

> Say: O Sir, how you generously offer the glass,
> Filled with tea that poets so commonly praise,
> So strong that it leaves in the glass a stain;
> Even after it's washed black markings remain.
> Then you pour fresh coffee over cardamom seeds:
> Coffee that stains with henna-red beads.
> And then when you bring your guests what to eat,
> Goat-ghee flows through the rice and the meat.
> Say: I want a young camel whose ride is a 'high':
> Tawny, not whiteness that glares in the eye;
> With a saddle and saddle-bags fitted just right,
> And tassels that sway between his legs when in flight,
> And a thigh-rest new, its thongs on his withers,
> And reins stitched by hands dyed a henna-red hue.
> If the king gave me only a pack camel-Fine!
> But speedy young mares set me on fire.

The poems of instruction are enchanting too, hovering around the recurrent theme of hospitality: the host must be overtly available to his guests, light a fire immediately, roast the coffee beans right and then dispense coffee correctly. He needs a spacious tent, a wife of good breeding, enough goats for fresh meat and enough camels for milk. And for power, that would in turn help him make a good host, a Bedouin needs brave sons, a good rifle and a high reputation.

Here is an example of a poem on the making of coffee:

> Roast me three handfuls, friend, one after one;
> Let the beans in hot ghada-coals waft to the mart.
> Take care that they neither be burnt nor undone;
> While roasting don't let yourself dream, but be smart.
> The cadence and beat of your grinding should stun,
> Even out in the waste, weary travellers will start.
> In a coffee-pot, tall by the fire, heap the grains;
> Then the pot, like a crane, will go round with a tray.
> The coffee, poured, will leave dark reddish stains,
> Like the blood of a sheep, heart and lungs cut away.

But for the likes of Clinton Bailey, all this would be lost to us.

From Easy Rider to Revolutionary

Browsing the bursting bookshelves at Blossoms, the Bangalore bookshop, I found myself hoping for a small miracle: that from the piles of tempting books, some priceless one that could not be denied would waft its way towards me. The miracle happened, in a manner of speaking: my hand fell on *The Motorcycle Diaries of Ernesto Che Guevara* and I knew I had a winner. These notes of an early journey across Latin America by the young medical student Ernesto—he would get the typical Argentinean nickname Che later—were not meant for publication. Thankfully, the notes did not remain only a sheaf of typewritten pages: the *Diaries* is a fundamental text that provides not only a lyrical, entertaining and insightful account of Latin America in the early 1950s but is also a record of the inward journey of arguably the most romantic of twentieth century icons, the guerrilla doctor whose trademark beret, long hair, beard and leather jacket have become synonymous with revolution.

The journey begins innocently enough: jaded by 'medical schools, hospitals and exams', the twenty-three-year-old Ernesto (or Che) and the older, out-of-work leprosy

doctor Alberto Granado decide to hit the long road on
Granado's 1939 500cc Norton bike, dubbed La Poderosa
II (The Mighty One). Che's parents worry that he is yet
to get his medical degree and he is asthmatic (the *Diaries*
contain sentences like 'The next day was uneventful but
asthmatic ...') but of course there is no stopping him. Any
young man who has set off on a long journey searching
for his guiding star in life will recognize the sentiments in
the early part of the *Diaries* ... the rush of the road, the
dusty miles flying by, the thoughtful quiet evenings in
strange places, the exchanging of confidences, the magic
of the unpredictable encounter ... Che's words capture
the typical youthful yearnings of the footloose: 'Distant
countries, heroic deeds and beautiful women spun around
and around in our turbulent imaginations.' And when he
and Alberto stare out at 'the immense sea, full of white-
flecked and green reflections', each far away with his own
dreams, two stowaways between places as evocative as
Valparaiso and Antofagasta, it's only natural that he should
write: 'There we understood that our vocation, our true
vocation, was to move for eternity along the roads and seas
of the world. Always curious, looking into everything that
came before our eyes, sniffing out each corner but only
ever faintly—not setting down roots in any land or staying
long enough to see the substratum of things; the outer
limits would suffice.'

The journey takes the two travellers from Argentina
to Chile and then up to Peru, Venezuela and Columbia

through mountains, deserts and rain forests. The narrative is not always intense; in fact for the most part it is racy and light-hearted, generously sprinkled with political incorrectness. Che alternates between being a political thinker and a poet and, when he is neither, he is just a young man having fun on the road; the two hitch-hikers are not above playing confidence tricks on strangers for a free meal, drinks and rooms.

As Alberto, who died not long ago in Cuba, would recall later, it was fortuitous that La Poderosa did not prove mighty enough; after a series of accidents and mechanical collapses, the bike had to be left in Chile and the knights of the road suddenly became two grimy, hungry hitch-hikers who continued their journey by truck, bus, steamship and raft. This threw them into direct contact with the people, brought them close up with poverty and misery. What could have been just another 'coming of age' journey before the inevitable retreat into bourgeois comfort turned out to be the political awakening of the man who would play a critical role in Cuba's revolution and in the Congo and would ultimately die trying to bring about a revolution in Bolivia, dreaming of the unchaining of all Latin America.

After talking to swarms of beggars huddled under dark staircases in Valparaiso, Che writes: '... we plumb the city's depths, the miasmas draw us in. Our distended nostrils inhale the poverty with sadistic intensity.' In the dying eyes of an asthmatic, poor old woman who can no longer earn her living with dignity as a waitress, Che 'comprehends the profound tragedy circumscribing the life of the proletariat the world over'. And then, on the way to the massive, exploitative, copper mine at Chuquicamata—a symbol of 'gringo' imperialism—his conscience is jolted by the sight of a persecuted Chilean communist couple: 'The couple, numb with cold, huddling against each other in the desert night, were a living representation of the proletariat in any part of the world.' The Indians of Peru evoke another political reaction from Che: '... these people who watch us walk through the streets of the town are a defeated race. Their stares are tame, almost fearful, and completely indifferent to the outside world. Some give the impression that they go on living only because it's a habit they cannot shake.'

On his twenty-fourth birthday—'the cusp of that transcendental quarter century, silver wedding of a life'— Che finds himself in an Amazonian leper colony. Drunk, or as he says 'piscoed' on the Peruvian drink pisco, he outlines his belief that the division of Latin America into 'unstable and illusory nations is completely fictional' and all the people from Mexico to the Magellan Straits constitute a 'single mestizo race'. When the two doctors finally leave on a raft down the river, the leprosy patients serenade them in a ghostly scene against the jungle, lamps reflecting in the river, an accordion player without fingers plays the instrument with little sticks tied to his wrist as he accompanies a blind singer.

It is no surprise that Che, having come so close to the misery of so many, has little doubt 'that when the great guiding spirit cleaves humanity into two antagonistic halves, I would be with the people. I know this, I see it printed in the night sky that I, eclectic dissembler of doctrine and psychoanalyst of dogma, howling like one possessed, will assault the barricades or the trenches, will take my bloodstained weapon and, consumed with fury, slaughter any enemy who falls into my hands ... I feel my nostrils dilate, savouring the acrid smell of gunpowder and blood, the enemy's death; I steel my body, ready to do battle, and prepare myself to be a sacred space within which the bestial howl of the triumphant proletariat can resound with new energy and new hope.'

So he wrote, so he lived and so eventually he died, blessed that life did not permit enough time for his ideals to corrode.

The Superfluous Man

It's the same space in the sky, but that's about it. The tall, straight-lined and right-angled Intourist Hotel, the pride of Soviet Moscow, once stood here, at the end of Gorky Street. I would wander to a lace-curtained café on its twentieth floor in search of fresh sandwiches and hot coffee. Or sidle up to its mezzanine where a cooperative staff member would happily facilitate prized tickets to the Bolshoi theatre, our friendship sealed with an inexpensive but exclusive gift of a perfume from a hard-currency store. It vanished, that world: Gorky Street became Tverskaya and the functional but unimaginative Intourist was torn down and replaced by the Ritz Carlton with its near-baroque luxury, its marbled floors and chandeliered ceilings and its cafés where wealthy men of the world smoke cigars and sip mellow brandies to the sounds of a tinkling piano. It's all very different now and I look for signs of the old: the street, by whatever name, still has two squares dominated by the granite visages of two Russian poets—the declaiming Mayakovsky and the pensive Pushkin—and from the terrace of a lounge I can still see the same view of the Kremlin walls lit up in the brittle cold night and the fabulously coloured,

ethereal onion-domes of St Basil's across Red Square. It's
futile to wonder when this world changed and how much,
and where did those thirty years go with their moments of
iridescent joy and their pointed regrets that simply will not
die away; it's easier to return to the book in my room.

It's not just any book though, but the first major Russian
novel: *A Hero of Our Time*, written around 1840 by the young
poet-novelist Mikhail Lermontov. Set in the mountains and
spa-towns of the Caucases and Black Sea region and strewn
with Byronic episodes revolving around love affairs, duels
of honour and military adventures, it remains a novel of
immense romantic appeal and fascination to this day. Not
least because its author, the young Lermontov, himself cast
in Byron's mould, died a year after the book's publication,
killed in a duel at twenty-six.

The early novel, to take first things first, is interesting
for its uncomplicated structure which in fact is a stringing
together of incidents, events and stories, all involving
the Byronic hero (or anti-hero), Pechorin, an upper-class
military officer based in the Caucasus. First, the narrator—
Lermontov himself—is told stories about Pechorin
by a fellow traveller, the veteran staff-captain Maksim
Maksimych, who has known Pechorin in the past. The
second perspective is offered by a brief meeting between
the narrator and Pechorin himself before the latter sets off
on a journey to Persia, only to die somewhere along the
way. The longest portion of the book comprises Pechorin's
diaries which Maksim Maksimych, heartbroken by

Pechorin's indifference, hands over to the narrator; and the latter feels free to publish them after Pechorin's death.

Pechorin typifies the 'superfluous man' of nineteenth century Russian literature, preceded by Pushkin's Eugene Onegin and followed by Turgenev's Rudin. This class of noble gentlemen, usually of high intelligence and ability, found themselves utterly helpless against Czarist autocracy. Burdened by a sense of boredom, cynicism and weariness,

they pursued idle intellectual or social interests. Some, like Lermontov, and his creation, Pechorin, tried to find an escape in frenzied activity—the military life, dangerous travels, romantic scrapes, gambling and duels. But the sense of world-weariness remained, heightened no doubt by the ability for self-analysis: 'My soul has been spoiled by the world, my imagination is unquiet, my heart insatiate. To me everything is of little moment. I become as easily accustomed to grief as to joy, and my life grows emptier day by day,' Pechorin mourns. And before going into a duel in which he may die, he muses: 'The loss to the world will not be great; and I myself am already downright weary of everything. I am like a guest at a ball, who yawns but does not go home to bed, simply because his carriage has not come for him. But now the carriage is here ... Goodbye.'

Pechorin's attitude towards love and women dominates the book. His whimsical obsession with and then disregard of a Tartar princess, his revival of an affair with Vera, his love of bygone years and his concomitant manipulations to win the love of Mary, a Moscow princess in a spa-town, are elaborately depicted. Pechorin comes through as a man who really does not care much for anyone but himself. As he admits: 'I often ask myself why I am so obstinately endeavouring to win the love of a young girl whom I do not wish to deceive, and whom I will never marry.' And then: 'To none has my love brought happiness, because I have never sacrificed anything for the sake of those I loved: for myself alone have I loved—for my own pleasure.'

He cannot countenance the thought of marriage for which he has the same unaccountable dread that some people have for 'spiders, beetles, mice'. He cannot love women of strong character; he believes he acquires—without endeavouring to—invincible power over the women he does love; and he considers himself a master of the paradoxes of the female mind. He deceives, he prevaricates and he despairs. He wonders if his sole mission is to destroy the hopes of others, whether he is just the 'indispensible person of the fifth act', in the manner of an executioner or a traitor. Life offers him one chance of redemption when Vera departs with her husband and he realizes that she would be lost to him forever. He rushes after her in insane panic but when his horse falls and dies, his passion too cools. 'I realised that to pursue my perished happiness would be unavailing and unreasonable. What more did I want?—To see her?—Why? Was it not all over between us?'

In a telling preface, Lermontov answered the shock of his readers that such a manipulative man could exist and challenged the assumption that his portrait was based on the author and his acquaintances. 'A Hero of Our Time, gentlemen, is in fact a portrait, but not of an individual; it is the aggregate of the vices of our whole generation in their fullest expression.' Little wonder that Albert Camus, another chronicler of world-weary men, chose to begin The Fall with these words.

Known more as a poet than a novelist, Lermontov is a

word-painter of memorable descriptions, such as this of
a dawn in the Caucasus: 'The dancing choirs of the stars
were interwoven in wondrous patterns on the distant
horizon, and, one after another, they flickered out as the
wan resplendence of the east suffused the dark, lilac vault
of heaven, gradually illumining the steep mountain slopes,
covered with virgin snows. To right and left loomed grim
and mysterious chasms, and masses of mist, eddying and
coiling like snakes, were creeping thither along the furrows
of the neighbouring cliffs, as though sentient and fearful of
the approach of day. All was calm in heaven and on earth,
calm as within the heart of a man at the moment of morning
prayer ...' For that last simile alone, read Lermontov.

Cold Courage of a
Godless Revolutionary

I was a young child in the early 1960s, watching the sunny afternoon street that ran past the amaltas tree in front of the house, when I was told that it was 23 March, the anniversary of the hanging of Bhagat Singh. I did not quite know what a hanging meant but I still remember the nameless and haunting dread that suddenly took over that careless afternoon. A second childhood memory recalls a 1965 front-page photograph of the garlanded body of Batukeshwar Dutt, one of Bhagat Singh's closest associates, under a banner headline: 'Batukeshwar Dutt Dead'. I had the impression that he had lived into hoary old age after being awarded life imprisonment. I now realize he was only in his mid-fifties when he died. All this was before the legend of the hanging of Bhagat Singh, Rajguru and Sukhdev was emblazoned emphatically in public consciousness by Manoj Kumar's superb *Shaheed*, a film which should be made compulsory watching for every Indian school student.

Recently, the first two major newspapers I scanned on 23 March only mentioned Bhagat Singh by way of two government-sponsored advertisements and quite another Dutt, named Sanjay, dominated the news columns. Mercifully the third newspaper—the one in Punjabi being read by my driver—rescued me from the precipitous edge of cynicism: it carried a front-page essay on the revolutionary.

Not only was Bhagat Singh a fearless patriot and one of the most charismatic figures of India's freedom struggle, he was also a thinker and an intellectual giant in the making when the gallows took him at the young age of twenty-three. Immersed in books from the Dwarka Das Library founded by Lala Lajpat Rai, since his childhood, he had developed a strong intellectual underpinning and political philosophy, strongly influenced by Marxist-Socialism, to his actions. His wide reading, his grasp of political ideologies and revolutionary movements sweeping the world and his vision of true revolution in India come through in the statements he made at his trials, in his letters and his articles. It is believed that during the two years in jail before his hanging he wrote four books, but these are lost. Thankfully, Bhagat Singh's selected speeches and writings have been edited by Prof. D.N. Gupta and brought out in a slim volume by the National Book Trust. Reading them is one way of paying homage to his courage and conviction.

The most substantive piece in the collection is his essay 'Why Am I an Atheist'. This essay was smuggled out of jail and published by Bhagat Singh's father after his martyrdom in *The People*, the magazine founded by Lala Lajpat Rai. Bhagat Singh had put down his ideas on God and religion on paper when asked by an old prisoner if he believed in God. When he replied in the negative, the old man taunted him that he would start believing when his end was near. Bhagat Singh argues against the insinuation that his atheism is an offshoot of any vanity that may attach to him because of the popularity of the trials; rather, he ascribes his conviction that there is no Supreme Being guiding the affairs of men to his deep study of the Marxist doctrine. As he writes: 'My previous faith and convictions underwent a remarkable modification. The romance of the violent methods alone which was so prominent amongst our predecessors was replaced by serious ideas. No more mysticism, no more blind faith. Realism became our cult.'

He stuck to his atheism in the most difficult circumstances even though he knew that 'belief softens hardships, even can make them pleasant'. He ascribes the invention of God to 'encourage man to face boldly all the trying circumstances, to meet all dangers manfully and to check and restrain his outbursts in prosperity and affluence'. He points to the myriad horrors of social and political exploitation to question the existence of a benevolent God and asks why such a being would create a world of 'woes and miseries, a veritable, eternal combination of numberless tragedies'. His cold rational courage has the feel of steel: 'I know the moment the rope is fitted round my neck and rafters removed from under my feet, that will be the final moment—that will be the last moment. I, or to be more precise, my soul, as interpreted in the metaphysical terminology, shall all be finished there. Nothing further. A short life of struggle with no such magnificent end shall in itself be the reward if I have the courage to take it in that light. That is all. With no selfish motive or desire to be awarded here or hereafter, quite disinterestedly have I devoted my life to the cause of independence, because I could not do otherwise.'

Similar clear-headed logic and conviction are evident in his statements before the courts and his letters. He left his home when his father arranged his marriage without his consent and wrote: 'My life has already been committed to a noble cause—the cause of freedom of India. For that reason comforts and worldly desires have no attraction in my life.' He was sixteen. In another amazing letter to the Punjab governor, he (along with Sukhdev and Rajguru) argues that since they have been accused of waging war against the King and detained as war prisoners, they have a 'claim to be shot dead instead of to be hanged ... we request and hope that you will very kindly order the military department to send its detachment to perform our execution.' He wrote to Sukhdev, who was contemplating suicide over life imprisonment, that such a step would be cowardice. As for himself, he awaited capital punishment, of which he was always certain, as a 'beautiful death', saying that 'when the fate of a country is being decided, the fate of individuals should be forgotten.'

But that is not the same as saying that a country, once its tryst with destiny is done, should ever forget such individuals.